MOVE TO AUSTRALIA?
YOU'VE GOT TO BE KIDDING!
A Moore Family Odyssey

Connie Moore

Belleville, Ontario, Canada

Move to Australia? You've Got to be Kidding!
Copyright © 2002, Connie Moore

All Rights Reserved. No part of this publication may be reproduced, stored in a retrieval system or transmitted in any form or by any means—electronic, mechanical, photocopy, recording or any other— except for brief quotations in printed reviews, without the prior permission of the author.

National Library of Canada Cataloguing in Publication

Moore, Connie, 1930-
    Move to Australia? You've got to be kidding! : a Moore family odyssey / Connie Moore.

ISBN 1-55306-438-0   LSI Edition 1-55306-486-0

    1. Moore, Connie, 1930- —Journeys—Australia. 2. Australia—Description and travel. 3. Navy spouses—Biography. I. Title.

DU117.2.M66A3 2002   919.4'045   C2002-905585-7

**For more information or
to order additional copies, please contact:**

Essence Publishing
44 Moira Street West, Belleville, Ontario, Canada K8P 1S3.
Phone: 1-800-238-6376. Fax: (613) 962-3055.
E-mail: info@essencegroup.com
Internet: www.essencegroup.com
To order: www.essencebookstore.com

Table of Contents

Acknowledgements 5
Special Thanks 7
Preface 9

  1. The First Step 11
  2. Packing Up 21
  3. One More Goodbye 29
  4. Welcome Aboard 35
  5. Bora Bora 45
  6. A Magic Island 51
  7. Mom Goes on R&R 57
  8. Next Stop—New Zealand 65
  9. We Have Arrived 71
10. Starting Out 79
11. Learning the Ropes 87
12. Crossing the Plain 97
13. We're Not Alone 107

14. Western Australia 115
15. Reverse Procedure. 125
16. Settling In. 135
17. A Special Visit. 143
18. An Australian Christmas 151
19. A Corner of the Bay 161
20. Mr. and Mrs. Farmer 169

Acknowledgements

THIS BOOK IS DEDICATED TO MY HUSBAND, Bill, and my children, Rusty, Mickey, Skippy, Tia, Pam, Jackie and Topper.

Many years ago, the idea of this book was planted in the heart of a young girl. Before the age of marriage and before children, I knew there was going to be a story. In the 1960s, I began jotting down events, feelings and "profound" revelations of life. These brief jottings and copies of lengthy Christmas letters are the backbone of *Move to Australia? You've Got to be Kidding! Book One*.

Birthed in the '60s, it began to emerge as a book in the '80s. Sadly, in our last move, it was buried in a closet. Oh, I talked about it, joked about it and dusted it off occasionally. But there was always something else that needed to be done. Yet the dream stubbornly refused to die. A year before our fiftieth wedding anniversary, I promised the children I would have it finished for our Golden Celebration.

It took an intense year, piecing together notes, receipts, photos and faded memories to complete the dream. Bill and the children graciously contributed by filling in the blank spaces—especially Bill, who was daily challenged with questions: "How many miles was...? How long did...? What was the name of...? until, finally, the book was finished. Together we lived it. Together we wrote it.

Because this family odyssey covers many years and numerous people, it is being presented in a series of four books.

Special Thanks

To Luther Yonce, who kindly volunteered to spiral-bind copies of the completed first draft. They were ceremoniously presented to my husband and seven children during the celebration of our fiftieth wedding anniversary.

To Jackie Caporaso, who took on the task of "red-penciling" that first draft.

To members of the "Writers of Ocala Workshop," who read the first draft and offered positive critiques at our weekly meetings. Their encouraging feedback kept me on track as the book grew from one book to a four-part series.

To artist Larry Duncan, who expressed in a sketch my concept of the book's cover.

Preface

IN THIS BOOK, I HAVE ENDEAVORED TO render the truth as accurately as possible. Even though this is my story, it includes many other people who played major or minor roles. In some cases, my interpretation of events will perhaps differ from another's perspective.

Dialogue and incidents are reported to the best of my recollection. Although I cannot be certain every quote is entirely word for word, the thoughts, ideas and circumstances of the story have been preserved.

—Connie Moore

Chapter One

The First Step

BILL DRAINED HIS COFFEE AND STOOD UP to leave. "We could settle in Australia," he said, deftly plucking a piece of leftover toast from one of the children's plates.

Surely he's joking, I thought. *This is one of those silly conversations. Bill is such a tease.* "Of course, dear, anywhere you want," I retorted, refusing to take the bait.

"Mom, can we go outside?" eight-year-old Mickey called from the hall. His well-timed distraction allowed Bill to wave goodbye and slip out the door. I sighed. Children seem to have a built-in radar that beeps whenever their parents are involved in an adult conversation.

"Have you made your beds? Brushed your teeth? Put away your pajamas?" I needed time to think about Bill's parting remark.

It was 1960. We were stationed at Atsugi Naval Air Station near Zama, Japan. Bill was attached to the Office of Naval Intelligence as an undercover agent. Travel was not new to us. Bill's navy career had provided opportunities to crisscross the United States and live overseas. We had enjoyed the tropical beauty of Guam, visited rugged mountains in the Philippines, and now Japan. But go to Australia? To live?

We had just three years before Bill was to retire. The question, "Where should we settle?" was uppermost in our minds. Last month, he had suggested Tahiti. I laughed to myself but said nothing. The years of travel had dulled our homing instinct. Our family and friends all lived in different states. Which state to choose was the challenge. As I pondered these things, Mickey poked his blond head around the doorway breaking into my thoughts. "Mom, my chores are done. Can I go to Susie's house?"

"Good job. Yes, you can go." I turned to gather up the dirty dishes, wondering why Bill kept talking about Australia. Of course! The light finally went on. In his job, he spent a lot of time at the Australian Embassy, and this month, Australia was the featured country in our library. The reading room had a charming display of cute koalas, bouncy kangaroos and native boomerangs. They were arranged among books extolling the wonders of Australia. I chuckled; koalas, kangaroos and boomerangs pretty well summed up my fourth-grade knowledge of the country. One thing I did know—Australia was a long way off. Surely Bill had been joking!

I shook myself back into the present; time to check on the children. Rusty, our ten-year-old, was sitting on his well-made bed reading a book. I noted how much he

The First Step

looked like his dad with the same red hair and freckles. As the oldest of our brood, he could be counted on to be a good leader for the others. He looked up. "Everything's done. Can I go out?"

"Will you be going down the street to play with your friends?"

"No," he huffed, looking annoyed.

"Why not?"

"All they do is watch television, so I'm just going to ride my bike."

"Maybe your friends will come out later," I encouraged. "Did Mickey come back?" Mickey, second in line, had a tendency to see things upside down and work problems out from conclusion to beginning—a confusing habit that kept us on our toes.

"He's playing with Susie on the porch," Rusty offered, putting his book away and reaching for his jacket.

"Where's Tia?"

"She's with Mickey," he said as he scooted out the door.

I didn't have to ask about Skippy. He was sitting on the floor beside his unmade bed playing with his little plastic army men. Six-year-old Skippy lived in a world of his own. As his dad often said, "Skippy belongs to Skippy."

"Come on," I offered, "I'll give you a hand with your bed." Sometimes, a helping hand works better than a scolding. Especially when you're dealing with a dedicated procrastinator. "There you go," I praised as he arranged his pillow. Ruffling his hair, I headed for the porch to see what was going on there.

I could always count on Mickey and Susie to come up with something unusual. Today, they had started a nursery school. "Very well set up," I said looking around at the supply of coloring books and crayons. They had borrowed the children's table and chair set from the kitchen for work space. Mickey explained the curriculum and the day's activities while he arranged story books and toys around the porch. "We still have openings available for new students," he assured me in his best grownup manner.

"We would be glad to take Teresa as a pupil," Susie said, using Tia's proper name. "It's twenty-five cents a day," she said primly. If they could keep a three-year-old entertained for even fifteen minutes, I'd consider it a great bargain. With a straight face, I enrolled our family princess, assured them of my payment and went off to the nursery to get Pam for her bath.

She was wide awake and demanding attention. Tiny for a three-month-old, Pam was full of spunk. Scooping her up, I whispered into her ear, "I think your daddy wants to take us to Australia, but I'm not going to let him." She acknowledged my resolve with a toothless grin.

The next morning, during our adult-conversation time, Bill quoted the average temperatures of all the main cities in Australia. He praised its wonderful climate. "Did I ever tell you I was in Brisbane during the war?" he asked.

"I think you mentioned it once or twice. Want some more coffee?"

He nodded, holding out his cup. "There's lots of room down there," he continued. "Most Australians own their own homes. They're a very friendly people, you know."

"Isn't it a long way off?" I asked. "That's where they have Aborigines living in the desert, don't they? I understand that everything is very primitive...." Heading for the hall without waiting for answers, I called over my shoulder, "I need to get Pam; she's fussing."

As I leaned over the crib to pick her up I confided, "Your daddy has always been a geography buff. He's interested because of those books in the library. It's just a whim. It doesn't mean we're going to Australia." Her blue eyes looked puzzled for a moment, then she wiggled and grinned as if to say, "Okay."

Bill and I agreed a farm was the only place to raise a large family. But where? Life in the States had become a "gimme-gimme" situation. We had noticed the growing trend of mothers joining the work force. Both parents were striving to provide their children with all the good things of life. It worried us to see nothing was required of the children to earn those privileges and possessions. We questioned the wisdom of raising a family without responsibilities. "How will they ever become dependable adults?" I asked. "Like frosting on a cake, they're only tasting the sweet."

"Life is more than the frosting," Bill said earnestly.

As the months passed, Pam became a little playmate for Tia while the boys were in school. It required both of us to keep track of this tiny dynamo. From the time she learned to walk at seven months, she developed a great curiosity about everything. One day, a lady selling books knocked on the door. As we stood there talking, curious one-year-old Pam lifted the hem of the lady's dress and peeked under it. Red faced, I apologized. The lady smiled stiffly and said it was time to go. "I was so embarrassed," I told Bill later.

He laughed. "What a way to get rid of a peddler."

Since his job required him to work odd hours, it was always special to have him home for dinner. One evening in

December, as we sat chatting over a second cup of coffee, he asked, "Would you like to go to Tokyo on Saturday?"

"That would be fun if Sachiko-san is able to babysit. Do you have anything special planned?"

"Yes," he answered glancing at me, "we've been invited to a Christmas party at the Australian Embassy."

"Oh," I said with a sinking feeling. He hadn't mentioned Australia for such a long time, I thought it had been forgotten.

Despite my hesitancy about the Australian thing, it was a wonderful evening. The people we met were warm and friendly. They assured us that Australia was the ideal place to live. "Mmm," I mused to myself. "Much as I love your accent, and as wonderful as your country is, Australia is still a long way to go."

Driving home, Bill asked me what I thought. "Well," I hesitated, "they were very nice, but I'm glad we don't have to make any big decisions this year. Our new baby is due in another month, and you'll be transferred soon after. That's enough to consider."

Bill reached out to hold my hand. "I hope it's another girl. That will give us three girls to go with three boys. A perfect half-dozen."

"I feel certain it will be a girl," I declared, "and I bet she'll have red hair just like you!"

Jacqueline Ann arrived the same week Bill received orders for duty in California. "How did you know she would have red hair?" he asked in awe.

"Mothers just know those things," I said smugly.

The children were thrilled with their new sister. Pam wasn't too sure about the change of focus, but she seemed to sense that "Jackie" would be her best friend and buddy.

The First Step

The next few months couldn't be called anything but hectic. The moving process is a major project in itself. But when a new baby enters the equation, the possibilities for turmoil are endless. We did manage to survive. The older boys were already seasoned travelers. They took things in their stride and provided wonderful help with the girls.

In April, we flew back to the States for duty at Miramar Naval Air Station. The green manicured lawns and flowering bushes, typical of California, were a stunning contrast to the somber colors of Japan. Our living quarters were lovely and new. For the first time, we had ample space for our family to be comfortable.

While we were unpacking, the boys went out to scout the area and brought back a full report. They knew where everything was located. "The movie theater is just over there," Rusty said pointing across the parade ground. Then, in unison they coaxed, "Can we go to the movies?" They had settled in. We were "at home" once more.

As the weeks passed we sensed a change in America. All around us we saw too much permissiveness and a lowering of values. The more children were given, the less contented they became. We knew this was not what we wanted for our children. We yearned for space, an opportunity to be a family unit, firm values and a work ethic. We wanted more than the frosting on the cake. But where could we find it? In Australia?

I leafed through Bill's accumulation of material on Australia. I read about the low crime rate, lack of juvenile delinquents and the high standards of free education. "What a contrast to the direction America is taking," I mused.

There were colorful brochures describing the world-famous Bondi Beach, Sydney's "coat-hanger bridge," the huge cattle stations in the outback and the opal mines at Coober Pedy. I read about Alice Springs, the town in the middle of nowhere. I devoured books by Nevil Shute, E.V. Timms, Arthur Upfield and poems by A.B. Paterson. Bill talked about flying doctors and Aborigines who could track anyone anywhere.

Australia—the land where the sun shines eight hours a day. Where it's not too hot, and it's not too cold. Where children are allowed to be children until they develop enough sense to grow up. A land of space and freedom to roam. A land for independent spirits.

We bought a recording of the song *Waltzing Matilda,* the Australian "sort of" national anthem. We played it over and over in fits of homesickness for a land we had never seen. Until—one inevitable day—the birth of a casual idea became a decision. We would go to Australia!

We told the children of our plan. They were delighted and accepted it as just one more move. The boys saw themselves hopping around with kangaroos. The girls were more interested in cuddly koalas. It all seemed unreal to me. That evening, sitting on the steps watching the moon, I leaned my head against Bill's shoulder. "Do you realize that we have always lived in an American environment, even in a foreign country?"

"That's right," he said quietly, "but this time we'll be the foreigners."

"How can we prepare the children?" I wondered. Sitting upright, I answered my own question. "I know! I could make scrapbooks with them. That will give them an idea of what to expect. Could we use some of your brochures and magazines?"

"Good idea," Bill said catching the spirit. "With all the information I've received from the embassy, there should be plenty for you to work with. Later, we'll take the children to the library to look for Australian story books."

A few weeks of glue-and-scissor sessions and lots of bedtime stories brought Australia alive to the children. They began to anticipate the journey. The boys, struggling with an overabundance of school work, considered it a great vacation.

Bill was relieved. "Now it's time to tell our families," he announced.

When they heard the news, they were stunned. Some of their first reactions were: "Take six children halfway around the world?" "Preposterous idea!" "How could you?" But gradually, they became resigned and slightly envious of our daring adventure.

Like the early pioneers of America, we had set our course. To Australia we would go.

Chapter Two

Packing Up

CAREFULLY, I MEASURED CHEERIOS INTO six empty peanut butter jars. I added milk and sliced banana. Bill tucked in a plastic spoon and handed them to the children. They were sitting on the floor with their backs against the wall. The table and chairs were gone. The house was almost empty.

I pressed my hands against my churning stomach. "Lord, am I going to throw up all over the place? How did I get myself into this?" It was May, 1963. Almost a year had passed since we made the decision to emigrate to Australia.

My thoughts flashed back over the past few months. The days and nights spent sewing clothes for the trip. A wardrobe of matching outfits for both boys and girls. Hooded jackets and bathing towels embroidered with their names. "I want people to be able to tell them apart," I explained to Bill. Summer clothes, winter clothes, play clothes, dress clothes... the task was endless.

We had given our living quarters a final polish—a Navy requirement for every move. We had been through the scrubbing and cleaning drill many times, but this was the last time. Bill had retired. No more Navy housing. No more Navy transportation—except to our final destination. After that, we would be on our own.

For weeks, preparing for the movers to arrive, we made plans as numerous and precise as a military maneuver. To have the essentials waiting for us when we arrived, the Navy allowed 700 pounds of goods to be shipped immediately. I made a list. Waving the list at Bill, I said, "Put all of these in the boy's bedroom. Tape a sign on the door in big print that says: 'Yes, pack.'"

We would need camping equipment for our trip across Australia. I made a list of camping gear to take aboard the ship as freight. I gave the list to Rusty. "Put these things in the girls' bedroom and tape a big sign on the door that says: "No, don't pack."

We would need personal luggage for eight people to hold both summer and winter clothes. We would be going from one hemisphere to another. I made a list. This one I kept for myself. Packing suitcases was my department.

"Mickey," I called, "I need some help. I want you to get all the suitcases and put them in my bedroom. Skippy, I need you, too. I want you to fill the wading pool for the girls. You can be my babysitter until we finish with the movers."

Pleased with his elevated status, Skippy paused on his way to the door. "Mom, do I get paid?"

"Yes," I smiled. "As soon as we finish, we all get paid with a big, fat, super-duper ice-cream cone." He grinned, yelled for the girls and was out the door. Give a nine-year-old boy a job dealing with water, and you can't go wrong... I hoped.

Everything else was to be stored by the Navy until we found a place to settle. The contract for storage read, "Not to exceed one year." Could we travel to a strange country, find work, hunt for the ideal location and set ourselves up in a year's time? *Too late to worry about that now*, I reminded myself. *We're not planning a picnic outing, and we can't change our minds if the sky looks cloudy.*

When the movers arrived, we took them on a tour of the house. We explained that the "Yes" room was to be a special shipment, the "No" room was not to be touched. I left Bill in charge of the proceedings while I made ice-cream cones for all the workers and, of course, Skippy and the girls.

By the end of the day, the house was bare except for the Navy-issue furniture and one room piled high with items to sort and pack. Bill and I looked at the room, looked at each other and nodded in an unspoken agreement. We had been married long enough to make decisions without words. After feeding the children, we put them to bed, left thirteen-year-old Rusty to keep watch and walked over to the movies. It's an art we've learned over the years; a few hours off for relaxation keeps us from blowing fuses. Of course, we would have to stay up half the night to make up for lost time. But unwinding the mind tends to oil the wheels of progress.

Gradually, order began to emerge out of the mountain in the middle of our set-it-aside room. I'm a slow, methodical packer who fills every inch of suitcase space and can put a finger on any item when needed—well, most of the time. I must confess, with each addition to our family, my reputation slips a little. Even so, there's a limit to how long one can hover over suitcases and trunks. Operating on the theory that everything looks better after a good night's sleep, we went to bed.

I was not prepared when the clock's alarm ushered in the new day. Did the morning dawn "bleak and cold" or "bright and sunny"? I wouldn't know. Sunny, I guess. All I remember is rattling around the empty house, muttering a litany of all the things that had to be done. The clothes dryer hadn't been sold… *ask Mary Jane if we can keep it in her garage.* There are times when presuming on a friendship is the only option.

Passing through the kitchen, I looked at my children sitting on the floor, eating from peanut butter jars. A fist closed tightly around my heart making it stop for a moment. I shook it off and went on with my mental list… *remember to give the peanut butter jars away; they come in handy. Dress the children in old, disposable clothes. Cram every last thing into suitcases—except the clothes we'll be wearing to board the ship! For heaven's sake, be sure that everyone has a pair of shoes. The sneakers they're playing in are only fit for the trash. Disposable sneakers: a great idea!* I grinned. My spirits were lifted by the silly thought.

Finally, we were ready. One last bit of wiping up in the house. One last look around in case we had forgotten something. One last parade to the bathroom. Outside, the rented station wagon had been packed to capacity-plus. With squeals and grunts, we squeezed in with the luggage and were off on our journey to a new life.

Packing Up

As we passed through the Miramar Naval Air Station gate for the last time, sixteen-month-old Jackie piped up from the back seat, "Bye bye, Miramar." There was a moment of silence before I heard a collective sigh. The sigh spoke of sadness for what had been and excitement for what was to come.

Settling into my seat, I asked Bill, "What's next?"

"We have a six-hour drive up the coast to Long Beach. We'll be staying with the Kings' tonight and board the ship tomorrow."

I smiled, remembering the Kings and their family of seven. "It will be nice to see Harry and Theresa again. You've known him a long time, haven't you?"

"Yes, I have. We met fourteen years ago. We were both stationed at Point Barrow in Alaska. It was just before you and I were married. Since then, we've often been stationed at the same base."

"Like Guam," I nodded. "That was the first time I met Harry's wife. I have never seen anyone tolerate life's trials as gracefully as Theresa. It must have been hard on her with Harry away in the Pacific for two years." I shook my head in wonder. "Especially with seven children to care for."

"That happens to men with certain ratings," Bill explained, "but it shouldn't happen in peacetime." Bill knew the frustration of being separated from family for long periods of time.

"Well," I soothed, "it's wonderful that Harry can be home with his family for a few years." I glanced at the scenery flowing by, and suddenly realized we weren't on the freeway. "Where did the freeway go?" I asked in surprise.

Bill chuckled. "Since I'm retired, I thought I'd take the scenic route. Might as well see the country while we can."

I looked closer. Could this be the California we had driven through for so many years? The old and the new passed pleasantly before us. Tiny villages tucked beside the sea. Quiet towns nestled in hills. Ultra modern, glass homes jutting out from steep hillsides. The children were so engrossed, they forgot to get restless—until we entered the roar of traffic heading into Long Beach. Suddenly, they were tired and hungry. "Which house is theirs?" was asked all the way up Ocean Boulevard and across town.

Finally, Bill pointed. "There it is, right there." By then, there was no mistaking their house. They had seen us coming. All the children poured out the door, followed by their dad who was barefoot and munching on a chicken bone. Harry is a man who knows the worthwhile things in life and isn't afraid to relish them.

While the adults exchanged "Hi's" and hugs, the children—all thirteen of them—streamed into the house chatting and laughing. *Would this good feeling last for twenty-four hours?* I wondered. It did. While the children played happily together, the adults talked about the past, the present and anxiously tried to store up sharing for the future. We knew that we would probably never meet again, but that was left unsaid.

Morning arrived too soon. In what seemed like a flash, it was time to go. Why is it there are so many things that can only be done at the very last minute? We went through the usual agony of: "Where's my belt?" "Which shoes?" "You haven't combed your hair." "What are you doing, pawing through that suitcase? You're messing everything up!" This was too much.

Finally, the dust cleared. My eyes settled on a whole flock of Cinderella magic-pumpkin changes. It's a pity they don't award medals to mothers for a campaign of this magnitude. Actually, it was as satisfying as a battle decoration to view the clean, well-dressed results: three boys in suits and ties and three girls in dainty dresses. After a last quick inspection and a round of fond goodbyes, we flew out the door. Settling into the station wagon, we focused on our next challenge—boarding the ship.

Chapter Three

One More Goodbye

WE LOCATED THE SS MONTEREY BY THE sea of people milling about. Some people were boarding. Some had come to say goodbye to people who were boarding. And others were there just for the excitement of it all. Slowly, Bill inched the car along the wharf to the loading area where dock hands quickly relived us of our mountain of luggage.

While Bill returned the car, I ushered the children up the gangway, urging everyone to stay close. On the upper deck, we were taken in tow by one of the ship's stewards. He guided us through the throng of people to our state rooms. Taking refuge in the largest stateroom, I closed the door and counted noses. "Thank goodness, we still have six children," I sighed with relief. But the safe feeling didn't last long.

"Mom, can we go look around?" Rusty asked with his hand on the knob and one foot out the door.

I nodded reluctantly. "Yes, but don't be gone long," I cautioned. What else can you say to a thirteen year old? I would have preferred, "No, you might get lost. Stay right here so Mama can keep an eye on you. Your mama is having problems enough without getting anxious about lost boys."

"They'll be fine," Bill assured me, arriving on the scene.

"Oh," I was startled. "Thank goodness you're here! Jackie is worn out. If you take Tia and Pam down to the other stateroom, I'll put her to bed." After good-night hugs and kisses, Bill and the girls left. I dusted Jackie off with a washcloth, put on her pajamas and tucked her into her crib. Slipping out the door, I walked down the corridor to the other state room. Bill was helping Tia and Pam get ready for bed. Trying not to sound anxious, I asked if he had seen the boys. "They were here a minute ago. I sent them to you. Oh, here they are, back again."

"Mom! we found the dining room," Rusty reported.

"And the swimming pool," Mickey added.

"But it doesn't have any water," Skippy said with a worried look.

They chatted on about the game area, the terrace and the movie theater. They had covered the entire ship and found their way back. Mom was relieved and quite proud. *I might survive this trip after all*, I thought.

"Boys, do you remember Mr. and Mrs. Szemenyei?" I asked. They nodded. "Well, they're planning to drive all the way from Pomona to see us off. Why don't you go out on deck and look for them." Off they went on their mission, full of excitement.

After we settled two sleepy girls in their beds, we eased out the door for a brief look at our surroundings. Streams of people crowded the corridors. Not able to get through the crowd, we finally retreated to the comparative quiet of our cabin. Bill closed the door, shutting out the noise. "I wonder if Barb and Steve will make it," he said.

"I hope so," I sighed, relaxing in the quiet of the room.

"Remember how we met on Guam?" Bill mused, stretching out on the sofa. "We had decided to have a quick swim before dinner."

"Yes, how could I ever forget? We went to Agat beach. On the way home you wanted to check the road under construction on Mt. Lam Lam. It was the last link in a road that would encircle the island. You were hoping it would be finished enough for us to go straight home instead of having to go all the way back around the island."

"The climb up the hill was all right," Bill said, "but the sand was deep along the top. We were okay until the car got stuck. I couldn't get it out." Bill shook his head remembering the frustration, the spinning wheels and the feeling of helplessness. Crawling under the car, he found the wheels hooked over a big log.

"And there we were," I reminisced, "hopelessly stuck, wearing nothing but bathing suits. It was almost dinner time, and the children were hungry. There was no way to get home except hiking down the mountain. I didn't really get scared until I looked over the cliff and saw those wrecked cars way down below us."

Bill picked up the story. "I remember carrying Skippy. He was two years old then. We had walked half a mile through the sand and Rusty and Mickey were already tired.

It was still another three or four miles to the village of Umatic at the foot of the mountain. It's a good thing you kept looking down over the cliff."

"I know! I couldn't believe it when I spotted movement way beyond the wrecked cars. I remember shouting, 'There are people down there. See them beside that black car?'"

"That's right," Bill said. "I tried to hurry everyone along, hoping we could catch them before they left. I was so relieved when they looked up and waved."

I laughed. "It's funny how casual we were. Waving hello to one another as though it were a common sight to see a family, dressed for swimming, climbing a mountain. I understood when we found out they had made the same mistake."

"Luckily, Steve and Barb had driven all the way to the bottom before they got stuck. Steve's friend was already on his way to Umatic to get help."

"The most wonderful part was the leftover fried chicken from their picnic at the beach. What a blessing. Barb apologized because it was all they had, but she didn't have to coax the kids to eat it. They were starved!"

"You can't help forming lifelong friendships when you meet under those circumstances," Bill said as his voice began to fade.

Hearing a commotion in the hallway, he jumped up and opened the door. There stood the Szememyeis. They hailed us with big grins, holding out a gift of pink champagne on ice. "I even brought tiny cups," Barb said as Steve popped the cork. We had a glorious party, conjecturing about the trip ahead and reminiscing about travels of the past. They were adventure lovers as much as Bill and I and vividly remembered driving us home from Mt. Lam Lam.

"That was just before we returned to the States," Steve said. "Isn't it interesting that, seven years later, we were lucky enough to be stationed in California, just a few hours from each other?"

"And now we have five children and you have six," Barb added with a chuckle. "That's what you call multiplication."

The announcement that all visitors must go ashore brought us up sharp. We said hurried goodbyes, keeping them light and gay. Parting from dear friends has happened so often, my heart would burst if I let the first tear escape.

As the ship slowly pulled away from the dock, we waved from the deck. Confetti and ticker tape fluttered in the air. The sights and sounds of goodbyes rolled over my emotions. I felt a quick pang of fear of the unknown that lay ahead and a strong urge to return to the security we were leaving behind.

Yet, we soon found ourselves awed by the panorama of the coastline's bright lights as they receded into the distance. We turned, relieved that we had passed another milestone. Hand in hand, we walked back to the cabin. It would be our home for the next three weeks.

Chapter Four

Welcome Aboard

"Mom, I'm hungry," a voice whispered in my ear.

"Okay, Tia, I'll get breakfast in just a minute." I opened one eye. It was still dark. "Why are you up so early?" I moaned closing my eye.

"The boat woke me," she said.

"Boat? What boat? Oh! yes!" The light dawned. We were on a boat, at sea and—I squinted at my watch—it was only 5:30. With last night's excitement of boarding, I remembered that none of us had eaten very much. I rolled over and nudged Bill. "Hon, Tia's starving. What do we do now? If Tia's hungry the others must be, too."

"Let's get everyone dressed," Bill mumbled, sitting up. "Then we'll go out to hunt for food."

We found the dining room. It was closed and not scheduled to open until much later. Just then the boys, our trusty scouts dressed and ready for the day, arrived with good news. They had discovered an early-bird brunch being served on the pool terrace. "Just what we need," Bill said swinging Pam up on his shoulders. I scooped up Jackie, and we headed for food.

Drinking eye-opening cups of coffee, we watched the sunrise and inhaled the salty air. Refreshed by the hearty breakfast, we were ready to tackle the day. We left the girls in the care of their big brothers and went down to organize our cabins.

We looked at the smallest room beside the laundry. "This would probably be best as the nursery," I suggested.

Bill agreed. "There's a crib for Jackie and two bunks for Rusty and Mickey. And there's extra room for storing suitcases."

"Wonderful. The boys will be here to keep an eye on Jackie, and they're already unpacked."

We moved down the hall to the much larger room with sleeper sofa, Pullman beds and crib. "This will serve as the family room, playroom and general meeting place," I said, tackling the rest of the suitcases. "Skippy will be good company for Tia."

"Don't forget Pam's net," he reminded me.

"My goodness, yes. If we found her in our kitchen playing with knives in the middle of the night, imagine what mischief she could do around here!"

Pam, a light sleeper, had discovered the night hours to be perfect for exploring places that were off-limits during the day. In desperation, I had cut a badminton net in two pieces and joined them with pink ribbons to make a square. At home, we used it around the lower bunk bed to keep her out of trouble. With it over her crib, she would be safe and secure aboard ship.

When we finished, Bill flopped on the sofa and picked up a brochure. "Want to know about your new home?" he asked. Bill loves factual information. He keeps me informed of all the details I don't have time to study and seldom remember.

"Give me the facts," I said, snuggling down beside him.

"Well," he said, "the SS Monterey is 563 feet long. It makes a six-week loop with Australia as its turn-around point. It carries 365 passengers, all in first class, and a crew of 500. According to the passenger list, there are fourteen children on board—six of them belong to us, the rest are teenagers."

I sat up abruptly. "Only fourteen children? You're kidding!"

"No. Haven't you noticed all the retired people around?"

"You mean we'll be on a ship with senior citizens for three weeks!"

"Yep! this is going to be quite an education for us."

"You're right. We haven't had much experience with older people. You just don't find many on Navy bases. I wonder how they'll react to the Moore bunch."

"Don't worry," Bill said with assurance. "It'll be all right."

"I hope so. But what if the kids don't behave? Before this is over, the captain might lower us overboard in a rowboat."

"Well, at least we're right next to the playroom," Bill mused, studying the floor plan. "That should help. Let's go take a look."

We rounded up Tia, Pam and Jackie to check on the playroom. Surprisingly, it was a very small room with a blackboard, slide and three little tables with chairs. I scanned the area with the sharp eye of a mother. "They bolted the tables to the floor in the middle of the room. There's no space for playing," I complained.

Bill ran his hand around the edge of the hexagon shaped tables. "Lots of corners for kids to bump into," he said, steadying Jackie as she wobbled. After one harrowing afternoon, we decided the playroom was no place for little children on an ocean-going ship.

"How are we going to keep them occupied?" I fretted. We don't want them to be a nuisance to all the senior citizens."

"I know a place to play," Mickey told us later. "Come, I'll show you."

The problem was solved when we discovered that the Polynesian Lounge, with its dance floor, was not used in the mornings. The boys rounded up empty cartons for the girls to play with. Little kids and cardboard boxes are a winning combination.

Our stateroom, beside the tiny laundry, was convenient. We put the clothes into a washer on the way to the dining room and into a dryer on the way back. One day, while I was waiting in line to get my laundry out of a dryer, the lady in front of me turned around. "Are you the mother of all those children?" she asked.

"Yes, I am," I replied tersely, not wanting to get involved in what might be an unpleasant conversation. Her next words left me speechless.

"They're adorable," she gushed, "and so well behaved. The boys take such good care of their sisters. They're always so well dressed, too. Your maid does a wonderful job." Noticing my raised eyebrows she asked, "You are traveling with a maid, aren't you?"

"No," I said, caught off guard. Inside I was thinking, *This can't be happening*. She was astonished that we didn't have a maid. She told me one more time how wonderful the children were and sailed off with her laundry. I collected my clothes and floated on air back to our cabin. *Don't get too cocky*, I cautioned myself, *the voyage has just begun.*

Evening meals were a real challenge. Breakfast and lunch served on the pool terrace were casual, but dinner was a dress-up affair. Food was formally presented with an elegant number of plates for each course. Tia and the boys adapted easily, but Pam and Jackie were famished and over-tired by the time we were seated.

"It's your turn to keep Jackie entertained," I told Bill, grabbing Pam as she tried to climb on the table. "Pam, here's another olive. Sit down, and I'll tell you a story." By the time the "real" food arrived, they had already dined on pickles, olives and crackers from the relish tray. As soon as the boys were through eating, they took the girls for a walk while we finished our meal in peace.

It was retired Colonel Baldinger who first eased my fears about the children. He took them under his wing like a benevolent grandfather. Pam, almost three-years-old, was a constant chatterbox but shy around strangers. She wouldn't speak at all if a strange person was nearby. She only began to relax during the last few days of our trip. Jackie, our dimpled redhead, was just the opposite. Everyone she met was a friend. The Colonel was delighted with Jackie's charm, and tried to help Pam overcome her shyness.

He enthralled the boys with his military stories. We often saw Skippy sitting in the lounge with the Colonel, completely absorbed in his latest tale. One day, he asked Bill, speaking with military briskness, "Did you know there's an Australian aboard ship? Name's Tom Barfield. Has a sugar plantation in Queensland, I'm told. Been visiting his brother in America."

We had heard of Tom Barfield. With his quiet Australian pleasantness, he was talked about aboard ship as much as we were. "G'day," he said when we finally met. "I 'eard yer goin' ta settle in Austrylia. Weryergoin?"

"After we land at Sydney, we plan to travel across the country to Perth," Bill told him.

"Fair dinkum?" he drawled. "I reckon Queensland in the East is the plyice to be." With a shy grin, he added, "It's a beaut country." Homesick for his four children, Tom became a part of our extended family. "Righto," he told the kids, "just call me Uncle Tom."

Another new friend was Annette Scheuermann, a New York secretary who loved to travel. She had left nieces and nephews behind and knew just how to make friends with little children. "Call me Aunt Annette," she said happily.

Flo and Marty Badaracco, a kindly retired couple from New Jersey, adopted all of us. "We have lots of nieces and nephews and love to be around kids," Flo explained.

I finally began to relax. "We have a wonderful extended family," I told Bill. "The captain may not drop us over the side in a rowboat after all. Have you met Dr. Hickman yet?"

"Is he the fellow with thick glasses who spends a lot of time writing?"

"Yes. He told me he's been in Africa researching a new book. It's about children and health. He asked me a lot of questions about chest ailments, chronic coughs and the best type of shoes for growing feet."

"Right up your alley," Bill chuckled.

"Really," I said, defending myself, "he seemed to enjoy getting some practical first-hand information. This afternoon he asked me if he could mention our children in his book."

"What did you tell him?"

I wrinkled my nose at him, "What do you think?"

"Tell me," he coaxed.

"I said, 'Of course you can.' Now let's go up on deck for afternoon tea."

"Sure thing," he said, laughing at my sauciness, "that's the high spot of my day. The kids are up there already."

When we arrived on deck, I noticed Skippy sitting quietly by himself. *Is he sick*, I wondered, *or perhaps in trouble?* I took a little cake and sat down beside him. He shook his head, declining the cake. "Are you all right?" I asked. "Is anything wrong?"

"Oh no," he sighed, "I was just waiting for the garbage to be collected, so I can throw it over the side."

"Throw garbage over the side?" I was concerned. "Are you allowed to do that?"

"It's all right," Rusty said coming up behind us. "The crew lets us. We do other jobs, too."

"Like moving deck chairs," Mickey added. "We get to clean up spills and lots of things. We're the crew's helpers," he said proudly.

Skippy's face brightened. "You should see the fish come to feed on the garbage. There are hundreds of them."

"Wow!" I said, relieved. "Let me know when you're ready. I'd like to see the fish." I glanced at Rusty, "Do you know where Tia is?"

"She's visiting with Mr. and Mrs. Badaracco. We left Pam and Jackie with Dad."

Five-year-old Tia got on quite well by herself, talking and visiting as she pleased. We hadn't realized how grown up and competent she had become. Trying to find her when it was time to dress for meals was our biggest problem. "Tia," I explained, "you have to be here on time to get ready for dinner. I can't always send out a search party to find you."

"I don't know the time," she wailed, looking at me with tears welling up in her eyes. Dabbing at the tears, I realized that, even with a watch, she wouldn't be able to tell the time.

"I know what we can do!" I said brightly. "Remember the timer we brought?" She eyed me curiously. "We can set the timer and put it in your purse." She looked puzzled. "The one with the doll face on it. The one I made to go with your blue coat." She nodded happily. "Then, when it rings, you must come back to the cabin."

She laughed. "I can do that." We didn't have to worry about search parties any more. The timer was all she needed. And she delighted in telling people what she was carrying in her purse.

One evening, Bill went down the corridor to put Jackie to bed while I relaxed with a book. My internal clock suddenly registered that he was taking a long time. *Could anything be wrong?* I wondered, trying to concentrate on my book. I jumped when Bill opened the door. He walked in with a strange look on his face. "What's the matter?" I blurted. "Is Jackie all right?"

"Yes, she's asleep, and everything's okay. But you're not going to believe what happened."

I put my book down. "Tell me," I said, relieved that my fears had been groundless.

"I was coming back down the corridor," he began, "when a lady stopped me. She said she just wanted to tell me how sweet and well behaved our children are. She went on and on. I had a hard time getting away."

I told him about the lady at the laundry. "It's nice that people like the children, but we'd better not get swelled heads. It might be too good to last."

Gradually, we were stopped more and more in the corridors. Thanking each person politely, we escaped to our room and hooted with laughter. "No children could be that perfect!" Bill said.

Surprisingly, we began to get earnest compliments from the crew. One day, the ship's photographer approached us. "I've had a lot of requests for your family picture," he said. "Would you mind posing for one?"

Perhaps we had achieved more as parents than we realized. In the meantime, we were meeting some wonderful people. They renewed our faith in humanity. Too often we had been told, "People shouldn't have large families. They require too much time and are too expensive." What a pleasure to meet people who still considered children a blessing.

Chapter Five

Bora Bora

"THE COLONEL CALLED ME A POLLYwog," Skippy protested, stomping into the stateroom. Bill looked up from reading the daily bulletin.

"I guess we all are, until we cross the equator," he said.

"How can we be pollywogs?" Skippy demanded.

"It's just a fun thing," I broke in. "Have you ever heard of King Neptune?"

"No," Skippy said, sitting down by my chair, anticipating a story.

"Well, there's an old, old myth about a king who is supposed to rule the sea. Sailors believed he could cause storms or prevent storms. They prayed to him before they went on voyages and especially honored him when they crossed the equator. Nowadays, when ships cross the equator, they have a party with lots of fun and tricks. Then they give out certificates to people who have never crossed the middle of the earth before."

"I have a certificate already," his dad said. "I crossed the equator years ago. Now, I'm a Shellback."

"How come?" Skippy asked, not quite understanding.

"That's the fun part," Bill said. "Before you cross the equator, you're called a pollywog. After the Equator Crossing Ceremony, you'll be called a Shellback. Crossing the equator is really a very special thing because not many people have that opportunity."

"Then you get to have cookies and ice cream," I said.

"Wow! I'm going to tell the other kids about this," Skippy declared, jumping to his feet.

"I'm glad you didn't tell him he may be thrown into the pool during the ceremony," I smiled.

"He won't mind," Bill said. "Let's take the girls up on deck. The ceremony is about to begin."

King Neptune was royally ushered in. He sentenced some pollywogs to a dip in the pool. Others were ordered to perform tricks. Rusty was squirted with shaving cream and had to walk the plank into the pool. Skippy and Mickey jumped in just in case.

"Where's my certificate?" Skippy asked, spooning his ice cream.

"It'll be delivered to our cabin before we get to Bora Bora."

With the activity of the equator crossing, not much had been said about Bora Bora. But now, a current of excitement ran through the ship. Passengers were busy signing up for tours and planning shopping sprees. Finally, the day arrived. We were nearing land!

We hurried to the pool terrace at half dawn to join others lined up at the ship's rail. Land was out there, somewhere. After looking at the ocean for a week, the prospect of seeing land was a big event. "There it is—Bora Bora!" someone shouted.

Bill scanned the horizon. "That's the French island where they filmed the movie, *Mutiny on the Bounty*," my information expert explained. "Bora Bora doesn't have docking facilities for large ships, so native launches will probably taxi us back and forth during our seven hours there. Let's get ready so we can go on one of the early launches."

We rushed to our state rooms to prepare for a day ashore. "You'll need your bathing suits and towels," I told the children. "Don't forget the camera," I reminded Bill as I packed a washcloth and change of clothes for the little ones.

Back on deck, we watched the anchor splash down as six launches, decorated with flowers and palm fronds, came to meet us. On the way to the beach, we made plans. "Tours are available," Bill said, "but Tom, Annette and the Badaraccos are going off on their own. They plan to visit the beach for a swim and picnic lunch and then go on to the village. Would you like to do that?"

"I'd rather to go to the village first, but since we have eight box-lunches from the ship and our beach gear to carry, it makes sense to do the beach first." When we docked, the boys climbed out of the launch and began to walk along the jetty. Skippy turned around and came running back. "Mom, Mom," he called, "my legs won't work right!"

"I know, Skippy. Mine don't either. It's because we've been walking on a rolling ship for so long. Pretty soon we'll get our 'land-legs' back again."

"It's funny," Mickey laughed. "I feel like I'm still on the boat."

As we strolled along, I was reminded of the three years we had lived on the island of Guam in the early '50s. The beaches, foliage and native houses made me feel right at home. Even the native boys, who materialized out of nowhere, were a familiar sight.

The white coral sand of the beach had a coarse texture, but the water was clear and cool. We settled in the shade of a large tree growing at the waters edge—a blessing for our tender, untanned skin. "Can Skippy and I go look around?"Rusty asked. Jackie was rolling in the sand, happy to be on solid ground. Mickey was testing the water with Pam and Tia.

Bill nodded yes. "Don't be gone too long," he cautioned.

We spent a relaxing two hours eating and swimming. The men worked at prying open coconuts that the children kept finding on the beach. Refreshed and rested, we gathered everyone together. It was time to leave. We gave the native boys what was left of the box lunches except the two that hadn't been opened. "Save those in case the children get hungry," Bill warned.

Tia clung to one small coconut. "I want to take it home," she pleaded.

"You'll have to carry it yourself," Bill told her. "We already have too much to carry." She nodded. When Tia decides to do something, she can be very determined. Tom and Marty lightened our load by carrying Pam and fourteen-month-old Jackie. Their little legs just weren't long enough to keep up with adults.

We boarded the truck for the village of Viatape. When we arrived, we discovered that, by going to the beach first, we had missed the folk singing and dancing. By the time we arrived, we saw only the native wares arranged on tables in a large hut by the jetty. "Can we buy something?" Mickey asked.

"We don't have room to pack anything big," I told him, "but you can each buy one small thing." We browsed among the native head dresses, grass skirts and beautiful shell necklaces while the children made their selections. The boys chose little, carved out-rigger canoes, and the girls decided on shell necklaces.

Ready to return to the ship, we trundled along the jetty, arms loaded with Pam, Jackie, box lunches and beach gear. I heard a moan behind me. "Oh no!" Tia cried.

I turned around, "What is it, Tia?"

"I dropped my coconut."

"Well, pick it up."

"I can't," she wailed. "It's in the water." Out of nowhere, a little native boy ran along the dock, dived into the water and came up holding the coconut. Smiling shyly, he handed it to a surprised but grateful little girl. She glanced at her daddy with a silent plea. Picking up on her cue, he passed the two leftover box lunches to the boys. "Now, that's a happy ending," I laughed. "The boys are happy with their prize, Tia is happy to have her coconut back, and Mom and Dad are happy because they have less to carry!"

Tired, dusty and wilted, we took the launch back to the ship. We were congratulating ourselves on arriving intact, when nine-year-old Skippy casually mentioned he had left his beach poncho behind at the bath house. This was not a casual situation! Let me explain.

Our children do not have ordinary clothes. Their wardrobes are designer-inspired, hand-tailored, original creations. Everything in sets of three. Three shirts for the boys, three dresses for the girls. A color-coded system that makes life simple. It's easier to keep track of what's dirty and what's clean. It's a cinch to spot three red shirts and three blue dresses in a crowd. Their bathing outfits were no exception. The boys had brown, Hawaiian-print trunks. I had trimmed their gold beach ponchos to match the trunks. As an extra touch to help people sort them out, I had embroidered their names on the backs. To lose one—disaster! Like breaking up a set of matched pearls! I looked at Bill who had been responsible for keeping track of the male side of the family and their belongings. He quietly departed for the purser's office.

The purser graciously radioed ashore. Happily, the beach poncho arrived aboard the last launch. All was well again with the Moore family, and tomorrow, we would be in Tahiti.

Chapter Six

A Magic Island

"DID YOU KNOW THAT TAHITI IS FAMOUS for its natural beauty and warm climate?" Bill announced, reading a brochure. It's the largest island of the French Polynesian islands. Papeete is the capital and chief port."

"Didn't they film the movie *South Pacific* there?" I asked.

"Yes, and *Mutiny on the Bounty*, but even before that, sailors always considered it a very special island. Every sailor I knew dreamed of visiting Tahiti one day. It has always fascinated me," he said with a far-away look in his eyes.

From the pool terrace, we watched Tahiti rising from the sea on a beautiful, clear Sunday morning. A customs officer who had boarded the ship, chatted pleasantly about his children and pointed out landmarks as we entered the harbor.

The gangway had barely touched the dock when beautiful Polynesian girls ascended to greet us. They wore sarongs and flower crowns on their heads. Their arms were draped with masses of fragrant leis to present to the passengers as a welcome to their island.

Will Rogers, the statesman, philosopher and actor once said, "Hawaii is the only place I know where they put flowers on you while you're still alive." It is also true of the island of Tahiti. I've never seen flowers used with such beauty and gaiety.

Uncle Tom joined us and offered to hold Jackie as we watched the ship dock. "Today is Sunday," he said, tickling Jackie under the chin. "As soon as the excitement of docking is over, a few of us are going ashore to find a church. Want to join us?"

"Wonderful idea. We'd love to." I turned to Bill, "Would you round up the children while I go below and set out their clothes?"

We hurriedly dressed, went ashore and asked directions to the church. "A little way up there," a native said, pointing straight ahead. We had no trouble finding the church, but it was closed. Puzzled, we asked a passerby. "This one closed. Repair," he said making pounding motions like a hammer. "Go on to town. See big building. Church there now." Following his directions, we arrived at a big building—and stopped.

Drawing close to each other for protection, we wondered if we were in the midst of an invasion. Sailors, armed with automatic weapons, lined the roadside and churchyard. What had we gotten ourselves into? We huddled in a small group, clutching the children, while Marty and Tom went to investigate. With relief, we learned that the sailors were an honor guard for the governor. "He be attending service celebrating feast day, Joan of Arc," a sailor told us politely. We were impressed, and honored, to be a part of this great event. We entered the improvised church and found places to sit on wooden benches. The sermon was all in French, but Jeanne d'Arc was mentioned often enough for us to be sure of the occasion.

On the long walk back to the ship, we decided to go native. "Let's stop in one of these shops to see what we can come up with," I suggested. Wandering through several little stores, we finally outfitted Mom and the girls with muu-muus, by far the most comfortable dress for the climate.

"Now," I told Bill, "we can look for sarongs for you and the boys. That's what the native men are wearing." That suggestion met with a chorus of "never!"

"I thought you were going to go native," I teased.

"Let's go check on the wide-brimmed hats," Bill compromised.

Looking very Polynesian with our muu-muus and straw hats, we were ready for the glass-bottom boat. It was beautifully decorated with flowers. As an added touch, there were hanging reed baskets full of hibiscus for ladies to wear. "Tahiti has everything," I told Bill, tucking a blossom behind my ear.

We spent the afternoon cruising the reefs and marveling at the plants and marine life that unfolded deep beneath us. Before we turned back, a native diver swam under the boat to put on a fish-spearing exhibition. The boys were thrilled. The girls were not impressed.

Back on the ship, tired but happy, the children reviewed their day. "I want a gun like that soldier," Skippy said.

"I want to go spear fishing," Rusty spoke up.

Mickey thought for a moment. "I want some dinner," he sighed. With dinner and baths taken care of, we tucked them into bed. The evening was for adults.

A group of us set out to experience Tahitian night life. We started at the elegant Hotel Tahiti where we watched a style show by local designers. Using Polynesian materials and motifs, they had created beautiful gowns that would be at home in any Western setting. We also saw a troupe of highly trained hula dancers. The Tahitian hula, with its faster tempo, was not as beautifully expressive as the Hawaiian hula. "I don't see how they can rotate their hips that fast," I was amazed.

"However they do it, they sure do it with terrific speed," Bill marveled.

From the hotel, we moved on to a place that remained open after all others closed. "It's best to limit your drinking to whatever comes in sealed bottles," Marty advised. For us, orange soda was the choice.

"I see a lot of familiar faces," I whispered to Bill.

"I think most of them are the ship's crew," he whispered back. There was no floor show, but we had a lot of fun watching the Polynesian girls dancing with their Western partners. No matter what the tune or dance, they eventually slipped back into their native hula, leaving their partner wondering what to do. As the evening wore on and the drinks flowed, we noticed that no one really cared.

"Time for us to go home. Let's go find a taxi." Bill, being a seasoned sailor, knew the best time to leave. Back on the ship, we sat on the cool deck watching others return from their merry making. "Well, tomorrow's your day," Bill said.

"That's right, my trip to Moorea! What a wonderful Mother's Day gift. You really surprised me. I don't see how you arranged that tour without my finding out. Imagine, a whole day away by myself. Just think! Moorea was the island they used for Bali Hai in *South Pacific*. The magical island of Bali Hai. I can hardly wait."

"Well, while you're over there having a great time, think of me once in awhile," Bill sighed. "I'll be alone with all the children."

"You can handle it," I said, giving him a hug.

Chapter Seven

Mom Goes on R&R

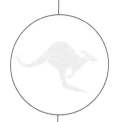

"ARE YOU JUST ABOUT READY?" BILL asked bright and early the next morning. "The kids want to walk down to the launch with you." After hasty, last-minute instructions of how to manage while Mom was gone, we hurried along the dock to the launch. I was decked out in my muu-muu and wide-brimmed straw hat and carried a tote bag with my bathing things.

"You look just like a tourist," Tia giggled, holding onto my arm.

"Don't forget to take pictures," Mickey reminded me.

"Here's the boat. It's called 'The Islander,'" Bill said, reading the name on the bow.

"Golly," I said, "it looks incredibly tiny compared to the Monterey."

"Don't worry," Rusty encouraged me, "it's big enough to get you there and back."

As I climbed aboard, I felt like a child being sent off to school. Waving goodbye, I called, "Behave yourselves," and went into the cabin to settle down for the trip.

"Hi, Connie," a voice said behind me. I turned around; it was Annette. "I didn't know you were coming on this trip. I would have waited and walked with you," she said.

"This tour is a Mother's Day gift from Bill," I explained. "But having you with me is going to be great. Imagine, only twenty people on this tour, and I already know one of them!"

As soon as we reached the breakers, we became fully aware that the launch was not equipped with gyro-stabilizers. Feeling queasy, we left our comfortable seats in the cabin and headed for fresh air. On the open deck, we joined those who had lined the rail, anticipating the first breathtaking look at the mystical island of Moorea.

In the distance, rising from the clear blue waters, we could see the volcanic mountains draped with a carpet of green foliage. Incredibly beautiful, they hovered serenely over Cook's Bay.

"Cook's Bay is known as the most beautiful tropical bay in the world," Annette murmured in awe.

As we drew near land, we saw a welcoming party of natives dressed in gay sarongs, waving from the dock. An outrigger canoe paddled toward us to escort us into the bay.

On land, we were presented with traditional flower leis and introduced to our hostess at the lodge. "Your day has been planned to include a swim in the lagoon, lunch, an afternoon tour of the island, a native feast and evening entertainment. But first, we would like to treat you to our welcome table," she announced with a lilt in her voice.

She ushered us into the dining room verandah to a table spread with a beautiful array of tropical fruits. I recognized papaya, melons, bananas and pineapples among other fruits that were new to me. The fresh pineapple was the sweetest I had ever tasted. I kept going back for more. "It's easy to see why people visit these islands and never leave," I told Annette as she heaped her plate a second time.

"I can agree with that," she said, nibbling on a chunk of coconut. After refreshments, we swam in the clear water of a lovely lagoon surrounded by emerald-green mountains. *No swimming pool could ever compare with this*, I mused, looking up at the clear blue sky with a smattering of puffy clouds.

At noon, a delicious lunch was served on a table sprinkled with flowers. Afterwards, we gathered on the lawn for a demonstration of the versatility of the coconut. We watched a native tear off the outer husk as easily as we peel an orange. He struck it on a pointed stake driven into the ground, ripping off an even wedge-shaped piece each time. My neighbor whispered to me, "The real trick is driving the stake into the ground without the aid of a single tool." I smiled. We had learned that at the beach on Bora Bora. Once the demonstrator removed the outer husk, he punctured the depressions on the top to let the milk drain out. For his next trick, he held the coconut in the palm of his hand, giving it a smart rap with a large, two-foot-long jungle knife. The result was two perfect coconut halves full of meat. I winced as I whispered to Annette, "Do that trick wrong, and you'd have two pieces of hand."

"Don't worry," she whispered back, "you'll never catch me doing any tricks with a jungle knife!"

We learned that the liquid in the ripe coconut was a rich milk used mostly for cooking, and that green coconuts have a refreshing, water-like drink. "A handy bit of information if you ever plan to take up jungle living," Annette commented.

"Don't worry," I whispered back, "I don't plan to."

We spent the rest of the afternoon touring the island guided by a saucy little Polynesian girl. Witty and full of interesting tidbits, she kept everyone amused. When we visited a vanilla plantation, she cautioned us not to touch the vines. "One blossom is worth a week's wage," she said. Later, we saw the place where the vanilla bean is dried and sorted for further processing. "Now that I know one bean is worth a week's wage," I vowed, "I'll never take another bottle of vanilla for granted."

Back at the hotel, we had one more dip in the lagoon before getting ready for a native feast. Dressed and ready, we were led to the cooking area to watch the pig being removed from the pit. It had baked all afternoon wrapped in banana leaves and covered with hot stones. Our guide explained that vegetables were also cooked in the pit. "And also," she chirped, "a pudding made from coconut milk seasoned with vanilla pods."

"Makes sense to cook it all in one oven, doesn't it?" Annette smiled.

"Right," I agreed, "especially if you have to keep a fire burning on top of it all afternoon so that the stones stay hot."

In the dining room, long, low tables were draped with banana leaves and decorated with towering arrangements of cut fruit. Our cups were freshly punctured coconuts set in bamboo rings to keep them from tipping over. The plates were banana leaves, the silverware—fingers!

"Thank goodness civilization has shown up in the form of paper napkins," Annette murmured, as we sat on reed mats, dipping our fingers into strange mixtures served in bamboo troths. I've always envied people who can enjoy food completely foreign to them. I cannot. I nibbled on pineapple and yams and consoled myself with visions of familiar foods waiting for me aboard the Monterey.

When dinner drew to a close, we were treated to a style show using the native sarong. I saw great promise in the variety of outfits that can be achieved by draping a few yards of material and tying a knot in just the right place. I thought of the mountain of clothes it took each week to keep our family properly dressed. I nudged Annette. "Do you think it would it be possible for sarongs to become a trend in our culture? All we would need is a few yards of cloth to dress the whole family." She laughed, shaking her head.

We ended our day on Moorea watching native dances by torch light. Our hostess explained the meaning of each dance. Was it a better understanding, or the natural setting, that made these untrained dancers much more enjoyable than the polished performers at the Tahiti Hotel?

As we walked toward the launch, Annette and I talked about our beautiful day. "I guess the quiet impressed me the most," she sighed.

"Yes," I agreed. "A whole world of quiet that you can feel seeping into your bones. No blaring TV, no radio static, no grinding washing machine."

She nodded. "The only sound of a car motor was our tour truck."

Perhaps I found the quiet even more noticeable because, on this unforgettable day without my brood, I was simply me.

Too soon, it was time to return to the real world. The homeward-bound sea rose in swells. The boat pitched and tossed. Rain sent us scurrying inside—but not for long. The stench of the gasoline motor and a handy plastic raincoat sent us back outside. Sitting on the hatch cover of the rocking boat, we breathed deeply. "Fresh air is best even if we do get wet," we agreed. A half-dozen sturdy souls joined us on deck. We sang songs and watched our guides do their never-ending hula.

Just as I was thinking, "This would be the place to live," I sadly discovered that the smiling, flower-bedecked Tahiti we see as tourists is not the every-day Tahiti. One of the guides explained, "Between ships, there isn't enough work to keep boredom away and sometimes not enough money to buy food." Tahiti, the beautiful island paradise that men have dreamed of from the time of Captain Cook's famous voyage, was suffering the pangs of a developing civilization.

On a lighter note, we were treated to the secret of dancing the Tahitian hula without dislocating our hips. "It all stems from the knees," the guide said, "if you can rotate your knees to rotate your hips, you can do the Tahitian hula." I filed this handy bit of information away for the future.

Even with all the gaiety and songs, I must confess there were moments when I wondered if we would ever reach land. A worrier by nature, I'm never sure how far a boat can roll before it tips over. No one else seemed to be concerned, so I decided panic would be rather out of place. But I must admit, the welcome lights of Papeete were wonderful to see.

It's sort of a mixed blessing, but I've always been able to leave the children for an hour, a day, or a weekend without clouding the event with worry. But on the trip back, I was hit full force by doubts, anxieties and frantic imaginings. No matter how long I've been away, or how short the distance, I find myself rushing up the last few steps to home. It's only after I've counted noses and know that everyone is okay, I can heave a sigh of relief and relax.

So, with anxious fears driving me, I rushed from the dock to our ship. Bill greeted me on the main deck with a worried look. A shiver of panic ran down my spine. "Rusty went deep-sea fishing with some of the crew," he explained. "He's in bed sick. I don't know what's the matter."

I started down the steps. "I'll go see him right away."

"Hon." Something in his voice jerked me around. "I can't find Skippy." Fear clawed at my throat! I stared as Bill continued. "He was playing on the dock, and now he's gone. I've hunted all over the ship for almost an hour. I'm just about ready to notify the authorities."

Calm, stay calm, Connie, my mind pleaded, but my heart was racing. "Where was he last seen? Who was he playing with this afternoon? Are they serving food in the dining room at this hour? Is there a movie being shown? Better check the theater anyway."

I rushed off to see Rusty. A mother's first reaction—check his temperature. No temperature. "What did you eat today? Were you out in the sun very much? Did you wear your hat?" Yesterday, we had bought him a straw hat wide enough to shade an elm tree. From his one-word answers, I presumed he had spent most of the day lying down, out of the sun, with only a drink of soda. Judging from the rocking of our small boat, I diagnosed sea sickness, an overdose of excitement, too much sun and mild dehydration. My mother's instinct, and years of experience, told me he would recover. "You'll be okay," I assured him, smoothing his forehead. Rest and drink this water. I'll be back pretty soon.

Now—where was Skippy? Hastily, I changed clothes expecting the worst and rushed down stairs to the dining room foyer to find Bill. I could see him in the crowd, coming up the steps. He was alone! My heart sank. As the people in front of him moved, I could see he was not alone. He was leading Skippy by the hand. His face had the expression of someone who had discovered gold in a tar pit. Blessed relief! My knees turned to rubber. I held onto the stair rail for a moment to steady myself. "Where was he?" I asked, taking Skippy's other hand.

"In the theater watching a movie. It wasn't listed in the day's events, but movies were being shown for Polynesian guests. I've already talked to him about the consequences of not letting me know where he had gone."

Skippy hung his head. I squeezed his hand gently. "We were so worried. What would we do without you? You must always tell us where you're going."

"I'm sorry," he said.

As my adrenaline returned to normal, I realized I was running on empty. Suddenly, I was famished. We settled the children and went to the dining room buffet. Over sandwiches and coffee, we traded stories of a day we would never forget.

Chapter Eight

Next Stop— New Zealand

WE WERE STILL IN BED WHEN RUSTY AND Mickey arrived with Jackie. "She was awake, so we brought her to you," Rusty said as she wiggled out of his arms and plopped onto the bed with a giggle.

"We have to go help the stewards move the deck chairs," Mickey explained.

"Move them where?" I asked, cuddling Jackie.

"We have to put most of them on the sunny side of the deck, so people can watch the sun come up."

"Mmm, sounds interesting. When you finish, let us know. We'll have breakfast and a swim."

"I'm going, too," Skippy said, trailing out the door behind them.

"I guess it's time to get up," Bill said with a yawn.

I rolled over and stretched. "It's tough

on parents when their kids have to go to work so early," I said, trying to be funny.

"I'm hungry," Pam announced, peeking out through the pink ribbons of her crib net. I lifted her out and tickled Tia awake. "Time to rise!" I announced. "It's going to be a great day!"

We dressed and joined the boys on the pool terrace for brunch. By the time we were finished, the morning was just right for a swim. Lolling on deck chairs to dry off, I sighed. "This is the life. Breakfast served by the pool and time to relax in the warm sunshine."

"And a pool to swim in," Tia reminded us.

"Enjoy it while you can," her dad advised. "When we left the States, spring had just started, but it'll be almost winter when we get to Australia."

Mickey counted on his fingers. "You mean, we have only eleven days of summer left?" he cried in dismay.

"That's right. Better make the most of it."

"If this is all the summer we get, I'm going to stay in the pool," Rusty said, proving his point by jumping into the salty water. Tia and the boys swam for hours. Pam, who had spent most of her three years in a swimming pool, was wary of this one. The water wasn't calm like the pool back home. It heaved and rolled with the ship and tasted funny when it splashed in her mouth. "Yuck," she said, wrinkling her nose, and refused to go back in. But she wanted to stay close while the others swam, so she occupied herself by climbing up and down the ladder to dip her toes in the water. Without realizing it, she was scaring the senior sunbathers into near heart attacks. "Please don't worry," I calmed them. "Her big brother, Rusty, is keeping close tabs on her. They've all spent a lot of time in swimming pools."

We didn't have to go far from the pool terrace for our next port. As the ship neared land, I stood at the rail watching a magnificent sight. Four rugged volcanic peaks stretched up from the skyline. "That's Rarotonga, the largest of the Cook Islands," Bill said, joining me at the rail. "The largest peak is over two thousand feet high."

"I've never seen anything so beautiful," I murmured, enthralled.

"Hey Mom," Mickey interrupted, still dripping from the pool. "The captain said we can't get close to the island 'cause there's no opening in the reef big enough for our ship. But don't worry," he assured me, "one of the crew told me the natives are coming out to us. They're going to sing and dance and have things to sell."

A heavy mist rolled in with the natives, but it didn't dampen the show or the shopping. It was a nice diversion, and by late afternoon things had returned to normal—well not quite. We had only four days of ship routine before our next port.

Having tasted the thrill of a foreign port, everyone was caught up in the excitement. New sights and sounds were waiting just beyond the horizon. Maps, touring lists and tips on shopping were exchanged. But a different kind of excitement stirred in the hearts of the New Zealanders. They were returning to their home and families.

Bill had arranged to take the boys on a tour of the island. It was my turn to babysit. "Do you mind staying behind?" he asked during our playtime with the girls in the Polynesian lounge.

"Not at all. Annette will be there to help you with the boys."

He nodded. "When she said she didn't want to go on the arranged tour, I told her we had room in our car since you were going to stay here with the girls."

"That worked out well for everyone," I agreed. "Have you planned a route?" I asked, knowing he had spent a lot of time with maps and brochures.

"Yes indeed," he said, swinging Jackie around. "We want to see everything: snow-capped mountains, rolling hills and the famous white sand beaches." In a more realistic vein, he added, "Well, we may not be able to do it all, but I do want to take that drive up Mt. Eden to see the extinct volcano."

"Me too, me too," Pam was pointing to giggling Jackie.

Picking her up and giving her a whirl, I cautioned Bill with a grin. "Watch out for those snow-capped mountains with volcanoes that might spit at you."

Bill laughed. "Afterwards, we'll go to a Maori village and possibly have time to go on to Rotorua to see the thermal springs."

"That's quite an agenda. I know the boys will love it."

We were standing at the rail next morning, holding Pam and Jackie as the ship cruised into the harbor. "Auckland is the largest city on the North Island," our information expert informed us.

Looking at the activity below as the ship tied up, I could sense Bill's impatience to get started. "As soon as I can, I'll rent a car for our tour. Are the boys ready?"

"I am." Mickey said. Standing at his dad's elbow, he was ready to go at a moment's notice.

Next Stop—New Zealand

"Great. Go find Rusty and Skippy, and tell them the gangway is going down." Mickey didn't have to look far. Rusty and Skippy were already standing by the gangway gate. As soon as the gate opened, Bill arranged for a car, and, with Aunt Annette, they were off to a new adventure.

I gathered the girls and went down to our cabin for a day of catch-up. The girls amused themselves with crayons and coloring books while I sorted things for the next leg of our journey. This would be our last day of quiet before getting ready to disembark in Australia.

After dark, I tucked the girls into bed and settled down to enjoy a book without interruptions. It was almost too quiet. My eyes kept straying to the clock. Where could they be? It seemed as though they had been gone for ages.

Suddenly, Skippy burst into the room, followed by Mickey and Rusty. "Mom! You should have seen the blood!" he said, wide-eyed and waving his hands in the air.

"Yeah, it was spurting all over," Rusty joined in.

I jumped up. "Blood? What blood? Where's Dad?"

"The cows," Mickey said, filling in the missing piece.

Just then, Bill walked in carrying the left-behind jackets and shoes. "What's this about blood and cows?" I asked, collapsing into a chair.

"Oh," he explained, "while we were looking at farms, we passed a herd of cattle that had just been de-horned. They were walking along the road still dripping blood. The boys were pretty upset until I explained what it was all about. I assured them the cows were going to be okay."

"What a memory to take away from such a beautiful country," I sympathized.

"I'm sorry," he shook his head. "Up until then, we had a great trip. The country was so clean. The farm houses were so colorful. It was a wonderful day."

"We don't want the boy's strongest impression of New Zealand to be bloody cows," I mused, passing out jackets and shoes to be taken care of.

"Why don't we tour by bus tomorrow?" Bill suggested after the boys went off to bed. I'm sure the girls would love being on dry land for awhile."

When we announced the outing in the morning, the girls were delighted. We started the day with a bus ride through the city. Bill was right. It was charmingly colorful and very well kept. When we arrived at the zoo, Rusty asked the handler, "Do you have any kiwi birds here?"

"Kiwis are nocturnal," the handler explained. "They usually sleep during the day, but I'll bring one out for you to see." Wakened from his sleep, the little kiwi wasn't feeling too peppy. But it was a special treat to see a real live kiwi, New Zealand's national symbol.

We went on to visit the War Memorial Museum. It houses one of the finest collections of Maori art and handicrafts in the world: beautiful ornamented objects inlaid with paua shell and jewelry made from a type of jade called native greenstone. We could have spent hours there, but it was time to go back to the ship. After a day of building good memories, we needed to make preparations for the end of our sea voyage. And, the beginning of a new adventure.

Later that evening, Bill and I stood at the rail, relishing our last night at sea. What do you think Australia will be like?" I wondered leaning against his shoulder.

"We'll see," he said, putting his arms around me.

Chapter Nine

We Have Arrived

BRIGHT AND EARLY, WE STOOD AT THE ship's rail, anxious for our first glimpse of the Australian coast. "There's land," Mickey said, pointing north.

"I see land over there," Rusty said, pointing south. "Which is Australia?"

"Both," Tom said. "We call them the Twin Heads. They're two points of land that mark our harbor entrance. We're almost home."

"Look! The coat hanger bridge!" the Australian passengers pointed excitedly at a huge bridge stretching across the harbor.

"That's our nickname for the Sydney Harbor Bridge," Tom explained as we sailed into the port of Woolloomooloo. Our Australian friends were home and, oddly, so were we.

As soon as the gangway went down, reporters came aboard with their TV cam-

eras. They wanted to interview us. "Why us?" I asked Bill.
"I don't know," he shrugged.

My stomach began to churn when they ushered us over to the TV camera. We were a news item. It isn't often people leave America to settle in Australia. The questions started: "Why did you come to Australia?" "Why did you leave America?" "Do you like it here?" *Now, that's a silly question*, I thought. *How can we know if we like it here? We haven't even landed.* The ultimate question was asked of nine-year-old Skippy: "Did you leave a girlfriend behind?"

After all the ridiculous questions, I began to feel sorry for myself. "We're so far from home and don't know anyone," I protested to Bill. Just then, I glanced over his shoulder and saw Tom holding Jackie up high so she could see his homeland. I swallowed, trying to relax. "We do know someone," I reminded myself. "It will be all right." Putting on my brave face, I smiled at the children. "Here we are, in Australia. Isn't that wonderful?"

But it wasn't. We were rushed out of our staterooms as soon as the ship docked. I spent an uncomfortable two hours in the lounge surrounded by suitcases and riding herd on the children. Bill spent an equally frustrating amount of time trying to arrange for hotel accommodations. "We don't have any available rooms," he was told. Finally, Dr. Hickman suggested an organization called "Travelers Aid." "They should be able to help you."

After a few calls, Bill came back with a relieved look on his face. "We're all set," he said. We breezed through customs with our twenty-two pieces of luggage and took a taxi to our lodgings. On the way, Bill explained that we had two rooms. "One for the ladies, and one for the men. That's the way Travelers Aid does it." At the hotel, he unloaded our luggage and paid the taxi driver.

Taking the girl's suitcases and mine, he led us up three flights of stairs in one of the most run-down places I have ever seen. Halfway down the corridor on the third floor, he stopped. "Your room is here," he said, unlocking the door.

By the time I realized just how bad it was, he had moved all our luggage in and paid for the weekend. Then he announced the rest of the news. "The boys and I will take our luggage down to the men's hotel. It's down the street a bit." He smiled weakly and turned to go. "Travelers Aid is just not geared to families." After he left, I sat in the room watching the girls. I tried not to show concern but wondered what would happen next.

After awhile, Bill returned. He had found a phone to call about the Volkswagen van. We had seen them in California. They were perfect for travel and camping. We called Australia and ordered one before we left the States. It was to be outfitted as a Kombi van with a large zip-on awning for a kitchen area. I jumped for joy when he announced the good news. The van was ready!

We happily looked for a bank where we could cash a check to pay for the van. "I'm sorry," the manager explained. examining our check, "this hasn't been made out to an Australian bank. It will have to be signed and sent back to the States to be verified."

"How long will that take?" Bill asked.

"About a week," he said apologetically.

I was devastated. "Could you suggest a nice, moderately priced hotel?" I inquired, hoping not to look as desperate as I felt.

"Lodgings are hard to come by this time of year," he shrugged, "but I'll make some phone calls." He disappeared into his office. After what seemed like ages, he emerged with apologies. "I'm sorry it took so long. I've found an inn, but it won't be available until tomorrow." We thanked him profusely and made arrangements to move in the next day.

Back at our room, I realized that, although the floors, walls and windows were dirty, the linen was clean with no sign of bugs. That was some comfort since we would be spending the night. "Goodness," I told Bill, "I didn't think we'd find out about being foreigners so soon."

"Different, isn't it?" he agreed. Trying to keep it light, he suggested we look for a place to eat. We walked down the street until we found a restaurant where we were able to get a scrambled egg for Jackie and pizza for the rest of us. The pizza arrived slightly burned on the bottom and was definitely not American style. For eggs, "scrambled dry" had a whole new meaning in Australia. But who cares when you're hungry?

Not wanting to go back to our room until it was time to sleep, we wondered what to do. "Righto!" (I had picked up a new Australian word). "Where do you go when you've no place to go?"

Tia piped up with a great suggestion. "To a movie."

"Good idea," Bill said. "Let's take a taxi to the downtown movie area." When we got there, we learned another lesson—good shows require reserved seats. We were finally able to get into a newsreel show. We sat for an hour, catching up on world events as though we cared at that point.

When Jackie became restless, we decided it was time to go back to our separate hotels. "I'll carry Pam," Bill said. "She's fallen asleep."

"Okay," I began to organize. "Rusty, you and I can take turns carrying Jackie. Mickey, you walk with Tia and Skippy. Tomorrow, Daddy will get the stroller from the luggage."

It had been a trying day. I was suddenly thankful to have a place to sleep, dreary though it was. Despite the rules, Bill insisted on Rusty staying with me to help with the girls. We all slept in one big bed, itching and scratching all night long. I told myself that the itching was caused by the starch in the sheets and not by some crawly creatures.

As I lay in the dark, my mind was in a turmoil. The contrast between shipboard luxury and our hotel room was overwhelming. I had promised to follow my man wherever he went, but this? Would I ever see him again? Did I really want to go through with this? Would morning ever come?

Thank God, it finally did. The girls woke up at 6:00, confused and wondering where they were. They brightened when I explained we were going out for breakfast. With Rusty's help, I had them ready by the time Bill arrived with Mickey and Skippy.

We put Jackie in her little canvas stroller and set out to find a restaurant. The weather was chilly and overcast. Even though Sydney was a bustling modern city, central heating was not a part of everyday life. "It's hard to believe this is the end of May," I said, shivering. I was freezing, and Pam had developed a cold.

The restaurant wasn't the best, but we did get some hot food. I managed to eat my first real meal since we landed in Australia. After breakfast, we took a taxi to the Thelellen Holiday Lodge. The advertisement read: "For tourists who enjoy superb modern accommodations at the world-renowned Bondi Beach." While it wasn't the Hyatt Hilton, it was comfortable, clean and sufficient. The beach was beautiful—a long expanse of white sand dotted with a few brave souls who didn't care that it was almost winter. Some were enjoying Bondi's famous surf. "That looks like fun," Rusty said wistfully.

"It makes me cold just to watch them," I shuddered. "Would you and the boys like to play on the beach with the girls?"

"Sure," he said. "We could build things in the sand, but I'd rather go play in the surf."

"Sorry," I said. "Just remember, keep the girls away from the water. Maybe you boys can swim later. The hotel clerk told Dad about a store that carries camping things and canned food. Stuff we took for granted in America is hard to find in Australia."

"It's okay," I told Bill. "The kids are having fun on the beach. We can go to that store to stock up now."

"Good," he said. "I need your help to choose the canned stuff."

"Why don't Australians use canned foods?" I wondered.

"I don't know. The clerk told me most people use either fresh or dried foods. Perhaps they don't have enough demand for the farms and factories America has. There are only about nine million people in the whole country."

"Look," I tugged at Bill's sleeve as we browsed through the little store. "Paper diapers. What a blessing. When we get on the road, there will be no guaranteed water supply for washing cloth diapers." When we left the store, I felt better about the trip. We had bought several packages of backup diapers to stow on the roof rack.

By the end of the week, we had the van outfitted—at least, as much as we could. The roof rack held our camping equipment from the States: a four-man tent for the boys, sleeping bags, an assortment of tools for emergencies, the large suitcases and the paper diapers. We also carried five gallons of water—just in case.

"You'll need to join the Royal Australian Association," the hotel clerk told us one day. "It's the equivalent of the AAA in the States." *Good advice*, we thought, driving into town. At the RAA we were able to get strip maps and lots of advice on crossing the Nullabor Plain.

Just as we were leaving, I spotted backpack travel bags for children. They were just right for holding pajamas, a change of clothes and personal items. I showed Bill. "These would give the children an opportunity to have their own personal things at hand, plus the responsibility of taking care of them. That would make it easier for me."

"Good idea," he said. "Having their own things will eliminate a lot of friction and give the kids a sense of security."

Back at Bondi, the children were thrilled with the backpacks. They scurried around, choosing their own special treasures to pack. "Tomorrow is the big day," Bill announced after dinner. "We're all ready to go."

What's the schedule?" I inquired of our semi-official tour guide.

"Okay," he said, reaching for his maps. "We're going to travel across the Nullabor Plain to Western Australia. When we get there, we'll settle near the U.S. Navy Base at Perth."

"I know that," I frowned, "but someone told me that going across the Nullabor with children is not a good idea. The road is not a super highway, they said. And they told me that over two thousand miles of it is unpaved. It's gravel road with few gas stations and fewer stores."

"Yes, but we've crossed the United States several times, and we're seasoned campers," he argued.

"But this is not America," I protested.

"We can do it," he said firmly.

Chapter Ten

Starting Out

IT WAS STILL DARK IN OUR ROOM AT THE Thellen Inn. I could barely see the calendar on the wall, but I knew the date—June 3, 1963. In a few hours, we would start the next leg of our journey: the trek across the desolate, unpredictable Nullarbor Plain.

It was much too early to be up, but I couldn't sleep. I wandered outside to our Kombi van. I shook my head and sighed gloomily. I should never have let Bill pick up the van and pay for it without me. Oh, he had offered to take me with him, but I had said, "No, you can manage." When did I forget that things important to women just don't register with men?

We had seen German Kombi vans in the States: split front seats with access to the back, comfortable car seats and a rear bench seat that folded down to make a bed. We called Australia and told them what we wanted. "We'll have it for you when you get here," they promised. How were we to know it would be jury-rigged over here?

I wanted to cry as I looked at the metal partition behind the front seats. There was no way to get to the back without going outside or crawling over the thirty-inch high partition. "That's okay for little kids," I muttered, "but what about big people like me?"

The back "seats" were two wooden storage bins with four-inch foam cushions on top. During our trial run, the cushions had crept forward with every bump on the road. They constantly needed to be hitched back into place. With the table set up for writing or playing games, it was difficult to keep from sliding under the table, cushions and all. The gas stove was attached to the side door. With the door open, it was convenient for cooking under the awning. When the door was closed, the stove was just above the tiny sink, making the sink useless during travel. The small gas refrigerator in the back storage area was difficult to reach without stopping the van and opening the rear door. I heaved a sigh of resignation and shrugged. "Too late to change anything now."

Hearing sounds of activity, I turned to go inside. The day had begun. The children would be hungry. Bill looked up from his campground directory. "I think I've found a good camping area. It's quite a distance, but we can make it if we leave before noon."

"Okay, you get the food ready, and I'll get the kids ready. Rusty, help Dad with the breakfast. Mickey, I want you to help me with the girls. Skippy, when we get the suitcases ready, you can take them to the van." The game plan was in motion.

After breakfast, the kids went out for a walk on the beach while we discussed our route. "Are we still going to Queensland first?" I asked.

"Yes, I would like to see what Tom's home state is like while we're here. We may never get back this way." He looked up and grinned. "The best part of being retired is: we can go where we want, for as long as we want."

By noon, we were on the road. We stopped here and there to look at plants, enjoy the view, or just to stretch our legs. The campground wasn't that far away, but with the rough roads it took longer than we had anticipated. It was dark by the time we arrived. "I don't feel like camping out," Mickey moaned.

"I'm hungry," Skippy complained.

"I'm tired," Pam whined, draping herself over my shoulder.

"All right," I said, rallying the Moore team spirit. "The quicker we get busy, the quicker we eat and go to bed." Bill zipped the awning onto the van for our kitchen area while the boys unloaded the tent and sleeping bags.

"What do you want me to do?" Tia asked.

"Would you entertain Pam and Jackie in the van while I get dinner? It's too cold and damp for them to be outside. After all, it's winter here."

"In June," Bill added dryly, passing sleeping bags from the roof rack.

Working together, we were warm, fed and ready for bed in less than an hour. We slept soundly, too tired to care about the unfamiliar surroundings. The next morning after breakfast, we walked around the campground to become familiar with the Australian terrain. As we passed a little bridge, Rusty saw a possibility. "Mom, can Skippy and I go fishing for awhile?"

"Do you know where your fishing gear is?"

"Yep, it's under the back seat."

"All right, don't go any farther than the bridge."

Mickey amused the girls while I scrubbed clothes in our tiny sink. Hanging up the last diaper, I looked up to see Rusty and Skippy sauntering into camp with their fishing gear. "The fish weren't biting but we had lots of fun," Rusty reported.

If being covered with mud was what he meant by fun, I had to agree. I realized that getting clothes clean and dry was going to be a big item on this trip. Picking up my bucket, I handed it to Rusty. "You got back just in time to do your laundry. Change your clothes and start washing."

"Aw," Skippy frowned. "If we have to wash our clothes, can we go back and get dirtier?"

"No," I laughed, shaking my head, "you're dirty enough already." Knowing their case was useless, they went to work with no complaints.

While the laundry was drying, we ate lunch out under the trees. I sighed, thinking of the things we had seen and done since we landed. "What?" Bill asked, knowing from years of experience I was about to utter a profound observation.

"I have an eerie feeling of having stepped out of a time machine. Australia is very much like America thirty years ago. Canned goods are costly and very difficult to find...."

"And, we have to remember to take shopping bags with us 'cause the stores don't have any," Mickey interrupted.

"I saw a TV at Bondi Beach," Skippy said, offering a good report.

"Yes," I agreed, "there are some signs of modern living. But even though automatic washing machines are becoming popular, hot water and modern bathrooms are unexpected luxuries."

Rusty grinned. "Central heating is a fire place, and air conditioning is an open window, but there's plenty of mud!" Little did we know how true that was.

Our next campsite was in a field, fifty miles from nowhere. We had driven all day without passing a store to replenish our food supplies. That night, we dined on rolled oats, cheese, potted meat (Australian for canned meat), bread and jam. Not fancy, but filling.

Sitting by the fire after dark, Bill and I talked about our camp set-up system. "It seems better than yesterday," I said. "Tia is doing well with the girls. She was having a hard time keeping Jackie off the wet ground until I remembered the stroller. It makes a handy high chair, too. Keeps Jackie in one place while we feed her. Are the boys working out all right?"

"Yeah, Skippy's a whiz at digging the latrine and garbage pit. Rusty and Mickey have taken over unloading and setting up the tent. Last night, I made the mistake of pitching it beside the van where the sink drains." He chuckled. "After sleeping in a puddle, they decided to set it up themselves."

"What a great revelation!" I laughed. "I'm glad the kids have jobs they enjoy doing; that leaves us free to do the mom and dad stuff." We sat quietly for awhile as the fire burned down. "I guess it's time to turn in." I said. I folded my stool and brushed mud off the canvas stroller.

"What happened to you?" Bill asked, noticing my limp.

"I've over-taxed my back sitting on those crazy cushioned seats, and a boil is developing on my knee. Every time Pam and Jackie climb over to the front seat, they land right on top of it. Oh," I sighed, "how I wish we had a split front seat."

"How did you get a boil?" he asked, ignoring the front seat remark.

"Who knows," I shrugged. "I suspect I lowered my resistance with all those wonderful desserts aboard ship. Ah! luxury does have a price. And, we're out of Vitamin C. As soon as we find a town, we need to stock up. Pam still has a cold, and we don't want it to get worse."

We broke camp the next morning under cloudy skies. We hadn't been on the road long when it began to pour and kept coming down. I sat up front in the more comfortable seat with the little ones to ease my aches and pains. The others played and squabbled in back.

Taking into account the colder weather and rough roads, Bill suggested we turn south to Canberra instead of trying to go north to Brisbane. "The weather news is not good," he sighed. We thought going south would be the best way to avoid cold weather. Right? Not when you're down under it isn't. Getting acclimated doesn't happen overnight. Innocently, we turned south.

By nightfall, we gave up hope of being able to camp and stopped at a restaurant to eat. After a good meal, we continued on to Australia's capital city. Canberra was renowned for it's beauty. "It was designed by an American architect," the Aussies told us with pride.

We arrived in pouring rain. Fortunately, we were able to get a cabin in a tourist park. The cabin had two rooms with table, chairs, ice box, five beds and a two-burner gas plate.

Unfortunately, the showers and water closet (WC for toilet area) were up on the hill. It was very cold and wet. Bill went out to get things off the roof rack. He came back in, looking whipped.

"What's the matter?" I asked, dreading the answer.

"Everything is wet," he sighed.

"What do you mean? The roof rack was covered, wasn't it?"

"It was. But the rain blew under the canvas."

I grimaced. Surely this was just a bad dream. Bill continued. "Everything on the roof rack is soaked. All the luggage is wet." Glancing at me, he added, "including the emergency supply of paper diapers." While I stood with my mouth open, he hurried on. "I went to the office. They told me we could rent blankets for tonight."

We checked out blankets and put the children to bed. There was nothing else we could do to make the situation better. We rolled into bed dirty, cold and damp.

Chapter Eleven

Learning the Ropes

THE OTHER SIDE OF THE BED WAS EMPTY when I woke up. I peered at Rusty sitting in the rocking chair, his jacket tucked around him for warmth, totally engrossed in a book. I leaned on my elbow and mumbled, "Where's Dad?"

"He went to the office," Rusty replied without looking up.

Shivering, I climbed out of bed, turned on the gas burner and heated water for coffee. It was ready by the time Bill walked in.

"I've been in the office listening to the newscast," he explained. "The good news first—we are a part of history in the making. This is the heaviest rainy season in thirty years. The bad news is—the rain has stopped but not for long, and it's very cold and damp outside."

We held a quick conference and decided to move to a heated room with bathroom and washing facilities. "They're hard to find in Australia," he cautioned, "but we can try. If we don't find a room, it would be best to head for a warmer climate, a creek and a campfire."

After breakfast, Bill went out to search and came back shaking his head. "No luck," he said. Discouraged, we packed up and started off. Thankfully, the sky showed signs of clearing. We opted to bypass Melbourne and go straight across to Adelaide, hoping for dryer ground. Another misconception. From noon on, we traveled flat, semi-flooded country. We couldn't even find a place dry enough to make camp.

A cloud of gloom was beginning to settle over us when Bill exclaimed, "Look! There's a sheep drover on the road." The children craned their necks to see. Pam and Jackie hastily crawled over the partition, plopping onto my lap for a better view. The drover was wearing a red kerchief around his neck and a wide-brimmed hat to shade his face. He ambled toward us, leading his horse. His dogs trotted back and forth beside him. Their eyes were on the flock of sheep nibbling grass by the roadside. A second drover brought up the rear.

Bill pulled the car off to the side for us to enjoy this truly Australian scene. While some of the sheep frolicked on by, others stopped to watch us watching them. Our sagging spirits lifted. Skippy happily observed, "If the sheep don't seem to care that their clothes are wet, why should we?" The children began to laugh and chatter. It was a good sound.

We had just about given up the idea of being able to make a fire to get things dry, when we spotted a small, sandy rise. The ground wasn't completely dry, but at least it wasn't under water. Relieved, we made camp and prepared dinner. We feasted on steak, potatoes and carrots with fresh apricots and grapes for dessert. In Canberra, Bill had discovered with delight that, in Australia, it's cheaper to buy steak than potted meat.

In the morning, we woke to more cloudy skies and not much hope of seeing the sun. While Bill cooked his famous pancakes, Rusty, our woodsman, started a fire. How he did it with only wet materials, I do not know. That's why we call him our "woodsman."

After breakfast, Bill checked the luggage. "The only suitcases badly soaked are the canvas ones," he said. "I'll string lines on the trees by the fire so you can hang things up to dry."

The kids busied themselves collecting firewood. Then they gathered sacks of pine needles to spread on the floor of the cooking tent so we wouldn't track mud into the van. Hours later, we discovered the best drying area was not above the campfire but around it. We busied ourselves propping up cartons and draping the clothes over them one at a time. While we worked, the girls played in the wet sand, getting dirtier by the minute. "It's unfortunate the weather is so cold and rainy," I fumed, "because we really are good campers."

"Maybe it will be better tomorrow." Bill was optimistic.

The next day, we passed through low, flat country with sheep on one side of the road and cattle on the other. The pastures were green and partly flooded. We saw a lot of water collecting along the roadside. The radio informed us that a small town we had passed through yesterday was flooded today. "It's a good thing we didn't find a room," Bill sighed with relief. "We'd still be there, cold and damp, with suitcases full of wet clothes."

"We are lucky," I agreed. "We seem to be moving just in front of the heaviest rains."

Late that afternoon, we stopped at a campground just outside of a town called Hay. Bill got out and checked the ground. "It's wet but not bad," he called.

I handed Jackie across to Mickey and climbed down to join him. "Do you think we can set up camp next to the river? If we could get close enough, we would be able to carry water from the river for washing clothes and taking baths."

"Good idea," he said. Let's look for the driest spot."

We chose our site and set up camp. Afterward, we hauled water from the river and heated enough for everyone to have a quick scrub-down. "Ah, bliss!" I cooed, putting on fresh, clean clothes. Modern conveniences like showers, tubs and washing machines are never more appreciated than when you don't have them any more. "But at least," I sighed with relief, "everyone's clean for now."

At 3:00 a.m., I awoke to the sound of rain on the roof. "What will tomorrow bring?" I wondered as I whispered a prayer. Bill and I got up at 5:30, while the girls were still asleep. The sizzle of sausages roused the boys, and I squeezed oranges to make juice.

Emerging from his tent, Rusty grinned. "The girls were really surprised when they saw you doing that the other day."

"It was funny," I laughed, remembering the looks on their faces. "They were really surprised to learn that orange juice doesn't always come from a can or out of the freezer."

For the first time in months, we ate quietly with the boys. The hectic days of entertaining little children during hour-long meals aboard ship were over. Just as we finished eating, we heard the girls stirring in the van. Another day of our odyssey had begun. I went in to help them get dressed.

We packed up during the periods when the rain slowed to a drizzle. For each camp, we allotted three hours to dress, cook, eat, wash-up and pack. The rain had started to come down steadily by the time we were ready to go. Overnight, the saturated ground had turned into mud. Bill climbed up in the van to move it. The wheels spun. We were stuck! "There's no one around to help us get out," I moaned, trying not to sound as scared as I felt. I'm fine if we travel a reasonably fair terrain. But any deviation in the form of mud, snow or steep mountains, turns me into a jelly fish. "What will happen now?" I asked Bill.

"We'll see," he said quietly. With everyone aboard, he skillfully rocked the van while the rest of us prayed. We lurched out of the rut and spun down into a gully, narrowly missing several trees. Crazily, we seesawed up the other side. My fingernails dug ridges in my palms. I held my breath. Skidding dangerously, we sped up a hill and onto the road. With my heart in my mouth, I breathed a heavenly thank you. The children yelled, "We made it!" We had reached the paved road, or bitumen as the Australian's call it. We were safe as long as we stayed on it—unless it disappeared under water.

Dull and uninteresting, the road stretched ahead for miles. Great pools of water stood in the fields and along the roadsides. Some fields were completely flooded. Around noon, Bill slowed down. Leaning forward in the back seat, I asked anxiously, "What's the matter?" I stiffened myself for bad news.

"There's a police barricade up ahead. Stay in the car," he ordered briskly. Getting out to investigate, he heard an officer explaining to a Catholic priest that the road was impassable. The priest told the officer he was going to Adelaide, and knew how to get around the flooded area. With this assurance, the officer nodded. "Righto, you can go."

Bill interrupted. "We're going to Adelaide, too. May we follow along?"

It was agreed. Bill climbed back into the van, and the officer waved us on. We started off through foot-deep water. But Bill was determined to stick close to our guide. There was no other means of direction: no visible roads and no road signs. The vista ahead looked like never-never land.

For over forty miles, we twisted through settlements of aborigine shacks. We splashed over fields covered with water, slipping, spinning and weaving to get traction. Bill's face was ashen. His knuckles were white from gripping the wheel. His eyes were riveted on the car in front of him. Suddenly, the van plunged through a ditch, skidded up a rise, and landed on bitumen! "We're on the road!" the kids shouted, releasing built-up tension.

Once more, Bill's skillful driving had saved the day! He heaved a sigh of relief. The color slowly returned to his face. "If we had lost that car," he said, quietly wiping his brow, "I don't know what I could have done. We would have been stranded with no way of knowing where we were or where we were going. I hope I never have to go through that again."

I hugged Bill and congratulated him on being such an excellent driver! We thankfully waved goodbye to the priest who had brought us through a very difficult situation. Does God send angels in times of trouble? Do they sometimes look like Catholic priests? We think so.

Learning the Ropes

By late afternoon, we had left the rain behind and were headed to higher ground. We camped dry that night and arrived in Adelaide the next day. Downtown, Bill pulled over to the curb. "I'm going to try the RAA to see if they will recommend a place to stay." He was back in a minute looking sheepish. "The office is closed," he said stiffly. "I had forgotten that from noon Saturday to early Monday morning, Australia comes to a halt."

"Where do you begin to look for lodging in a city of this size?" I asked. To answer my own question, I pointed to a man with a broom. He was sweeping the sidewalk outside the ladies' comfort station. Politely, he directed us to the Salvation Army a couple of blocks away. They sent us to a camping area six miles away. The camping area had no washing machine and no heat. They sent us on to another campsite that wasn't suitable either.

Downtown again, we stopped at a place called the Travel Lodge, a very nice motel with an RAA rating. They were booked by a convention but sent us on to a guest house. Adelaide was a dignified city with fine old homes. Many of them had been turned into guest houses. "Just what we needed all along!" I crowed. "A guest house is the nearest thing to home. They usually provide washing machines, drying areas, hot baths, ironing facilities...."

"And breakfast!" Mickey finished.

We were given one large, high-ceilinged room with five single beds. "Will five beds be enough?" Bill asked me.

I shrugged. "We'll make do." It was such a relief to be there. The room wasn't heated, but we were accustomed to that by now. I unpacked all the dirty laundry and went off to find the washing machine. The lady of the house led me to the backyard wash house. Since I was a foreigner, she carefully explained how things worked. "Fill the copper and light the gas burner under it."

"Copper?" I said.

"Yes, Ducks, 'tis the tub next to the washer."

Going back to the room, I asked Bill, "Do you know about coppers? I need you to light one in the wash house and fill it up for me. Then you have to put the hot water into the washer."

"I'll see what I can do," he said. "Come on, Skip, this sounds like fun."

They went out to light the copper and heat the water while I sorted a load of clothes to start with. I carried them out to the wash house. "We're just about ready," Bill said, pouring another bucket of hot water into the washing machine.

"Oh, good. Everything is so dirty. But, with this copper business, I know I can't get it all done today."

"It'll be okay," Bill said, putting his arm around me. "Comforts we've always taken for granted are bound to get scarcer as we head west."

I tried another Australian word. "Too right!" I said as I loaded clothes into the tired, old wringer washing machine. When it started grinding away, we went in for lunch.

That evening, we took turns savoring warm baths, another interesting experience. The bath water was heated by gas as it ran through an enclosed coil by the tub. "That's efficient," I told Bill. "You only heat what you use instead of keeping a whole tank of water hot all the time."

"But you only get hot water in the bath tub," Bill reasoned, "unless they have another heater in the kitchen."

"It's still a good idea," I insisted.

The next day, Bill and the children went exploring after church. They came back from their walk all excited. "We found a park with swings and slides," Tia shouted.

"I went down the slide all by myself," Pam boasted.

"Me too," Jackie grinned, lifting her arms for me to pick her up.

"It's a great park," Bill said. "We just happened on it. Do you want to go back with us to see it?"

I smiled, balancing Jackie on my hip. "I think my 'sightseeing' is going to be the backyard wash house. My 'recreation' will be getting everything fresh and clean for the next part of our journey. Actually, I enjoy learning about Australian living. Especially wash houses and coppers." The idea of being "thrilled" about wash houses and coppers tickled my funny bone. I burst out laughing.

Bill looked at me with concern. "Are you all right?" he asked.

"Sure," I said, trying to compose myself. "You watch the kids, and I'll get the clothes done.

"Okay," Bill sighed. "Let me know if you need me. In the meantime, I'll be keeping the kids busy at the park."

Chapter Twelve

Crossing the Plain

CLEAN AND DRY, WE LEFT ADELAIDE AND drove on through South Australia. As we passed cultivated farmland bordering on a gulf, our well-informed tour guide pointed out, "That's the Gulf of St. Vincent which empties into the Indian Ocean."

"Golly, Dad," Rusty said, "could we stop somewhere near the water? I want to be able to say, 'I was in the Indian Ocean!'"

"Sure, we're coming to a place called Port Pirie; we'll stop there."

"I'm getting ready, now," Mickey said, taking off his shoes and socks. The others followed his lead. Just outside of Port Pirie, we found a park by the water. Bill pulled over. The boys burst out of the van and began to run. "Don't get your clothes wet," I called after them.

Skippy was the first one in, "Wow!" he yelled. "It's cold! How wet do I have to get to say I've been in this ocean?"

"Oh-oh," Rusty shivered. "I think up to the ankles will do it."

"Just imagine," Mickey said, as they dried off, "I'm only eleven, and I've been in three of the world's oceans. Only two more to go."

"Yeah," Rusty said, "the Arctic and Antarctic. Maybe we'll get to wade in those one day."

"Not me," Skippy said, pulling on his socks. "If they're as cold as this one, I'm not interested."

Nearing Port Augusta, we found a most unusual campground. It had kangaroos, emus, cages of birds and a playground. After so many muddy campsites, the children were thrilled. "Real live kangaroos!" Mickey exclaimed, climbing out of the van.

"Hey! Emus!" Skippy shouted. "Can I ride one?"

"Not today," I said firmly.

"Look, swings!" Tia cried, running toward a swing set.

Holding up her arms to be lifted onto the swing, Pam squealed, "Mommy, swing me!"

Jackie toddled toward her dad. "Me too," she cried.

While we were pushing swings, Rusty, the explorer, showed up with a report. "Did you know, there are a lot of people here because the road to Alice Springs is flooded?"

He was right. Later we talked to a couple traveling by bus with four children. "We were travlin' to a station up north, beyond Alice Springs," the sad-faced father explained. "Word come down that the road's washed out up thar. Now, we have ta wait for it ta clear."

In the friendly manner of the outback, his wife gave us the address of a cousin in Perth. "He's a retired farmer," she said. "When you get to Perth, look him up and say 'G'day' for us."

We met another lady who had come up from Port Lincoln looking for her daughter. "My daughter went up to Alice Springs with her aunt and uncle in a caravan." She paused. "I think that's what you Americans call a trailer." I nodded. "On the way back," she continued, "they got bogged down in the wet." I looked puzzled. She paused again. "The 'wet' is when we get rain and everything floods. It only happens every four or five years," she explained. "It's good to have the water, and everything blooms for awhile. But it can be tricky."

She went on with her story. "They had to spend four days without any fresh water. They boiled water from mud puddles to survive. It was all they had for drinking and cooking. When they got here, their caravan was covered with red mud. But we're happy they got through," she grinned. We chatted for awhile longer, wishing them good luck on their trip back home.

As we wandered away, I breathed a sigh of relief. "Boy, am I thankful that we weren't caught in the flood." We could have been. I had my heart set on visiting Coober Pedy. It was an opal-mining center. Most of the people lived in underground houses cut into limestone hills. I wanted to see those houses. I wanted to get one of those opals. Unfortunately, Coober Pedy was on the way to Alice Springs.

"Time for a conference," Bill said. "The road to Coober Pedy is too dangerous to travel."

"I have to agree," I sighed wistfully. "What should we do now?"

"Well, I was going to swing down around the peninsula to Port Lincoln, but under the circumstances, that might not be wise. It would probably be best to cut across the top of the peninsula to Ceduna. It's the only town of any size this side of the Nullarbor. But," he hesitated, "I've been told that the road is unpaved and rough. What do you think?"

I shrugged. "Could it be any worse than what we've already traveled?"

We decided to follow Bill's plan and started out the next day. As we passed Iron Knob, we stopped to pick up a hitch hiker. "G'day," he said in a heavy Australian accent. "Oym goyn' t' Strykie Biy." He was joining a road crew there. Their job was to seal the road with bitumen, he explained.

"We're on our way to Ceduna, if that will help," Bill told him, not sure where "Strykie Biy" was. I couldn't understand half of what he was saying. While he talked to Bill, I searched my map to find a place called Strykie Biy but could not find it.

We arrived at a little town called Poochera. "I'll be getting off 'ere," he said, gathering up his sleeping roll. "There'll be a ride 'ere t' tyke me to Strykie Biy." After we dropped him off, we passed a sign pointing to a side road. It read, "Streaky Bay." Remembering his accent, I realized that Streaky Bay was indeed his destination. Amazed at this new accent we would have to learn, I nudged Bill. "Hon, Strykie Biy is Streaky Bay."

"You could have fooled me," he said.

"They" were right about the road to Ceduna being unpaved and rough. It was indeed—full of potholes and occasionally under water. Progress was aggravatingly slow. We could travel fifty miles an hour only on the stretches that had been recently graded. We blessed every graded mile. As we bumped along, I told Bill, "I envy the people who'll be using this road after our hitch hiker gets it sealed."

"Don't feel too bad," he said. "It could be worse. The rains are right behind us. In three more days, we probably wouldn't have gotten this far."

That night we pitched camp just outside Wirrulla. We tried to buy eggs. We couldn't. "They're jolly scarce this toyime o' year," we were told. Same story with fruits and vegetables. But we found a hearty two-pound loaf of unsliced whole-wheat bread, the kind grandma used to make. Quart of milk? No. "Tyke your pitcher up to the big barn on the hill." We were told. "They'll fill 'er up right from the dyiry can."

We were setting up camp, when Mickey called. "Dad, come see these critters. What are they?" They were about as big as rabbits with long, narrow, pointed heads. Their tails looked like rats' tails. They had been scratching for bugs but disappeared into burrows when we arrived.

"I bet they're bandicoots," Rusty said. "I read about them. The mother carries her babies in a pouch like a kangaroo."

"Can we dig them out?" Skippy asked.

"I don't think that would be wise," his dad said. "Let's finish setting up while Mom gets dinner."

The next morning, by the time we struck camp, everything was soaked with dew. While we were packing up, we churned it to mud and took a lot of it with us when we left. It clung to our shoes, clothes and equipment.

As we drove on, towns became much smaller and many miles apart. Some of them housed only the butcher, baker and garage owner. No "Quick Stops," no "Zippy Marts." Eventually, towns thinned to a petrol pump and one small store. I began to hear complaints from the back seat. "This is boring," Mickey said.

"Jackie's eating my crayons!" Tia complained.

"There's nothing to look at," Skippy moaned.

The road was like a roller coaster. Each time we topped a hill, we saw the same sight. The red ribbon of unpaved road spread before us with neither tree nor house. "Okay, let's play a game," I suggested. Guess how many miles to the top of the next hill."

"That's easy," Tia said, "it's forever miles."

"I think it's five miles," Skippy guessed.

"You're crazy," Rusty scorned. "It's at least ten miles."

"We'll see," I said. "Mickey, you can keep score. Whoever wins can decide what we have for dinner." The game kept us absorbed as the hours passed.

"Who won?" I asked Mickey when we drove into Ceduna.

"I think Tia did. She chose 'forever miles' on every hill. I can't argue with that. It did seem like forever."

Rusty and Skippy shouted, "We agree."

"I want pancakes," Tia said, remembering the prize.

Bill went into the little store and asked for pancake mix. "Sorry, we don't carry that," the clerk said. Hunting for a substitute, Bill heard her remark to another lady. "These city people come in here and ask for the craziest things." Tia had to settle for scrambled eggs and potted ham with a promise of pancakes when we reached Norseman.

We set up camp just off the road. We were beside the huge pipeline that delivered water from the Murray River to the West. Sitting by the campfire, Bill asked, "Could we start early tomorrow? We'll be passing through two Aboriginal reserves. Usually they have signs that prohibit motorists from leaving their cars. I don't know if that's to protect the Aboriginies or the travelers. But I want to be beyond them when we stop for the night."

"Jolly good," I said using one of my new Australian expressions. "We can do that. The kids won't mind an early start. They're all excited about seeing real Aborigines."

Getting ready for bed, I noticed car lights approaching. "Hon," I called, there's a car coming along the road. It's the first one we've seen for days."

Slowing down, the driver shouted, "Hello! We saw your lights. Is everything all right?" We assured him that we were just camping.

"Wasn't that thoughtful of them?" I marveled. Bill nodded in agreement. I went to bed comforted that we were among friends and not just lone campers in a strange land.

The next morning, we were off to an early start. We sailed along comfortably, on a bitumen road, through grain and dairy country. "Maybe we've passed the worst," I ventured. My optimism was premature. By noon, the pastures and green fields were replaced by salt brush and mulga trees. The road became a rough, graveled roadbed.

"The sealed road we just left must have been because of the town," Bill said. "The next 700 miles are the 'real' Nullarbor Plain."

"Where are the Aborigines?" Skippy worried as we drove through the first reservation.

"I don't know," Bill said. "Perhaps they're working on some station."

"You're silly," Tia said. "There's no train station here."

"Dad means a ranch," Rusty informed her.

"Yeah," Skippy said, "like cowboys and Indians. Only here it's cowboys and sheep."

After a whole day of anticipation, we had seen only a sign warning us not to leave our car. We passed through the second reservation just as the sun was going down. "I guess we aren't going to see any aborigines," Mickey said sadly. "There were lots of them in our Australian books. It's not fair," he pouted.

"If we did see any, they would probably look just like us," Rusty told him. "I bet the real ones with body paint and spears live up in the Northern Territory."

A little way beyond the reserve, we found a big enough clearing in the salt brush to set up camp. I looked around. This was desolate country. The only sign of life was a station house far away. There was not even a tree for our clothesline.

Dinner was late, and everyone was famished. I opened the back cupboard to get pans for cooking. "Oh no," I moaned, "everything is covered with dust! How could so much dust filter up into one cupboard? I'll have to use some of our reserve water supply to wash the pans before I can cook." Thinking of the water supply, I realized we were down to our last diaper. More precious water to do laundry. It was a comfort to know that, besides the tank of water connected to our sink, we had an emergency five-gallon tank on the roof rack.

We had been told that going off the main track and running out of water could fatal. Recently, a family of five had run out of gas and perished on the Birdsville Track in Queensland. They had neglected to tell the authorities

Crossing the Plain

where they were going and weren't found until a week later. Stories like that did nothing to make me feel secure. But at least we weren't on the Birdsvill track.

There was no time to worry. Pam and Jackie were over-tired and over-hungry. After going to bed very well for two nights, they just couldn't settle down. Jackie was fussy with a cold. The others may have sensed my uneasiness with the isolated campsite. It was after 8:00 before the little ones finally dropped off, and the older ones went to the tent to crawl into their sleeping bags.

The evening had been warm and calm, but during the night, a strong wind blew. It whipped up the canvas and banged the ropes against the van. I sat up abruptly, wide awake. I shook Bill. "What's going on?" I was turning into a jelly fish again.

"Maybe it's just a willy willy," he said.

"What's a willy willy?"

"That's what Australians call a whirlwind," he explained. "It will be all right. Don't worry."

"That's all right for you to say," I grumbled. I lay down but couldn't relax.

In the morning, the wind was still blowing. I was ready to pack and run. "Shouldn't we leave right now and eat later?" I asked Bill impatiently.

"Where could we go?" he said, rolling up a sleeping bag. "There's nothing out there, no towns—nothing. We'll be all right," he said calmly. "Let's have some breakfast." Food won out. But it was a hurried meal. We ate, washed up, packed up and were off by 7:30. A record for us!

I looked behind as we left the campground. A beautiful sunrise was lighting the sky. It seemed to be following us, blessing our day. I turned around to face the desert. To my surprise, in the distance I could see snow-covered hills. "How could that be?" I asked Bill.

Chapter Thirteen

We're Not Alone

BILL LOOKED AT ME AND SMILED. I could tell he had been studying but wasn't going to enlighten me just yet. "That's probably Eucla Pass," he said casually. "It's on the border between South Australia and Western Australia. We'll be there pretty soon."

"Mommy, read me a story," Pam pleaded, climbing over the seat and dropping onto my lap.

"Me too," Jackie chimed, scooting over the seat and snuggling down beside us. I forgot about the hills of snow and concentrated on *Bunny Tales*.

"Here we are!" Bill exclaimed, interrupting the story. He pulled over to the roadside. "It's as close to the ocean as we'll get. We all climbed out to smell the salty sea breeze and imagine what it would be like to see an ocean again.

Our next treat was the patch of bitumen road laid down to help motorists climb the steep grade over the pass. When we reached the top, we looked out on the ocean bordered by house-high, white sand dunes. "Oh," I exclaimed, "those are the hills of 'snow' I saw this morning! They're beautiful!"

Bill chuckled. "Wait until the next stop."

When we reached Eucla, Bill pulled over as close to the sand as he dared. "This is it," he said. "Early in the century, Eucla was a telegraph station on the long trek across the country. Gradually, the creeping dunes turned it into a ghost town."

The town had disappeared. But we found a path of inverted, empty beer bottles that led us to a house. Bill peeked into the only window. "I can see a desk and chair over in the corner. It's almost covered with sand," he said. We all took turns peering into the room.

"I would hate to have sand piled up in my house," Tia said mournfully.

"I hope it didn't bury people. Did it?" Mickey asked.

"No, it happened slowly. The people gradually left," Dad explained as Jackie wiggled to get down. He lowered her onto the sand. She giggled, plopped herself down and rolled in it.

"This looks like a great place for a snack," I said. I'll get some things from the van. Sitting on the sand with the warm sun on our backs, we munched on cheese and crackers and inhaled the refreshing ocean breeze. I silently stored away the moment. The sun, sea and sand of Eucla Pass became one of my favorite memories—a refreshing pause on our long trek across the continent. Ahead of us lay four hundred miles of unpaved Nullarbor Plain.

For the next seventy miles, the highway ran between a bluff and the ocean. We couldn't see the ocean, but we could hear it's roar. The bumpy road was full of treacherous potholes. We slowed to forty miles an hour and concentrated on every inch of road. But we still hit potholes with almost spring-shattering thuds.

"Mom!" Tia exclaimed, sitting in the front seat with me. "What's that fence doing in the middle of the road?" We had entered cattle country where it was common to see fences across the track.

"It's a stock fence," Bill said, slowing down. "Because of the lack of water-holes, cattle are allowed to roam large areas. Some of these roads go through cattle stations." He looked over his shoulder at the boys. "Who wants to open the gate?"

"I will," the boys shouted in unison. They jumped out, opened the gate and waited until we passed to shut it. Opening and closing cattle fences became their main source of entertainment. The road grew progressively worse. As we drove on, several herds of grazing sheep crossed in front of us. Then there were long spans of mud and water that had to be forded.

Five miles out from Eucla Pass, we came upon an aborigine driver. His truck trailer had broken down. He asked us to relay the message to a man pulling a car somewhere up the road. "If you happened see the bloke," he said.

"That shouldn't be a problem," I reasoned. "Considering the lack of traffic, they'll probably be the only cars we see."

Twenty-five miles later, we found his friend by the side of the road. A young, bearded Australian was stretched out comfortably on the seat of the first car. He waved and said,

"G'day." A good-sized dog appeared from behind the car, obviously keeping an eye on things.

Bill hailed the young fellow. "Your friend is about twenty-five miles back with a broken spring." While they talked, I followed the stockman's gaze as he looked back down the dusty, rutted road. I couldn't comprehend why he took the news with such a casual "Righto." Eventually, I came to understand. It's just the way life is out on the Plain.

A few miles later, we spotted another car in trouble. It was a blue Nash Rambler. We had passed by each other many times during the last thousand miles. By now, it seemed like an old friend. "We have flywheel trouble," the driver explained. "Could you take a message to the nearest garage? That would be Madura, sixty-two miles away."

"Sure thing!" Bill answered, happy to be a part of the fellowship of the road. As we started off, he explained to the kids, "The golden rule—'do unto others as you would have them do unto you'—makes a big difference out here."

Rusty leaned over the seat. "Did he say sixty-two miles to a garage?"

"That's right," Bill replied. "I read that only about thirty cars a day pass along this road. How about keeping an eye out for the sign to Madura."

Almost two hours later, Mickey shouted, "There it is!"

Bill swung off the highway onto a narrow dirt track. "I hope this is the right way," he mumbled as we bumped along. "It's been almost two miles. I don't see any sign of a town."

"Look, there's a house," Skippy pointed up a little hill. We discovered that Madura wasn't really a town; it was a homestead. It had a garage, petrol pump, a house and several other buildings.

"This is the way things are out here," Bill explained. "When there are no towns, these homesteads are the only connectors along the highway."

Apparently, the driver of the Nash Rambler had sent other messengers ahead of us. "Help is on the way," we were told. The trip to Madura wasn't wasted, though. The ruts and potholes had taken a heavy toll on our roof rack. It was broken on two corners. We had it welded back together, paid a hefty price for gas and pushed on.

Near sundown, we stopped just beyond Cocklebiddy. It was close enough to civilization to get fresh, pasteurized milk—in cartons! To celebrate, we broke out our extra five-gallon water can. Everyone had a sponge bath and the wonderful luxury of clean clothes. "Remind me to fill the can before we leave," Bill cautioned.

It was sprinkling when we packed up the next morning, just enough to clear the air, but not enough to settle the dust. With over 260 miles to Norseman, we faced another long, dusty day on a gravel road that reached endlessly over the horizon. Suddenly, Bill jammed on the brakes. "Will you look at that!" he said. A shaggy, bearded fellow was standing right in the middle of the road. He seemed to have come out of nowhere. He flagged us down. "Would you mail a letter for me when you get to the post office?" he asked. We assured him we would. "It's to my family," he said, stepping back so we could pass.

As we started off, I looked back. "There's no one there!" I said. "Where could he be?"

"Goodness," Bill said. "There's no habitation, no horse or car in sight." We had no idea where he had come from or where he went. Speculating about the possibilities kept us entertained and helped to pass the time. "He certainly was trusting," Mickey said.

"Why couldn't he mail the letter himself?" Tia asked. We found the answer to that question over 200 miles later when we finally reached a post office.

Concentrating on avoiding the deep mud holes, we didn't see the caravan approaching until it was fairly close. A man leaned out the window, motioning us to stop. "G'day," he said. "My wife and I are traveling across Australia. We just wanted to chat and catch up on any news you might have." When they realized we were Americans, they told us about their daughter who lived in Washington, D.C. "Perhaps you know her?" they asked.

"No, but if we meet her," Bill promised, "we'll say 'hello' for you."

We chatted on, exchanging opinions on the road conditions, coming and going. We told them about the floods we had passed. They told us we could look forward to a lot more water up ahead. Not good news, but the visit was a nice break in the day's monotony.

Later, we met a mother with two little children in a Volkswagen. "I'm on my way to Belladonia," she told us. Since our higher van commanded more visibility, Bill offered to lead the way. By now, we had slowed down considerably. We were churning through dust that filtered into the van, covering everything with grit. At times, we forged through water that might have concealed holes big enough to swallow us—not to mention the little Volkswagen behind us. We waved good-bye to them at Balladonia and stopped for gas.

Leaving the town, we found a spot to eat just off the road. As the children stretched their legs playing running games, another Volkswagen passed by. Surprisingly, it turned around and came back. A young man stepped out and joined us for a chat. "I'm traveling around Australia," he said. He was traveling alone and had specially outfitted his Volkswagen to make the circuit. "I saw your family and had to stop to say G'day," he smiled. "Have you just crossed the Nullarbor?"

"Yes," Bill nodded. "We're on our way to Perth."

The young man was amazed that an American family would travel across the Nullarbor Plain—with six children. "Could I take a picture of your family to remember you by?" he asked.

We obliged. Bill and I picked up Pam and Jackie, lined the others up and smiled at the camera. "I'm sorry we look so scruffy with all the dust and mud," I apologized, wondering how he would describe us to his friends.

In parting, he left us with some very good news! "The bitumen road starts just eighty miles this side Norseman," he said as he waved good-bye. We rejoiced. Only a few more miles of dust and ruts! Like water to a man in the desert is bitumen road to a traveler crossing Australia. It's discussed avidly around campfires, and each additional mile is written up in the news papers. Beginning eighty miles before Norseman, it flowed westward to Perth 450 miles away.

When we reached the paved section of road, the air suddenly became clear and crisp. The trees and shrubs were greener. Marvelous clumps of wild flowers were blooming along the roadside. They were as beautiful as the sweet relief blooming in my heart. By the grace of God, we had made it this far!

Chapter Fourteen

Western Australia

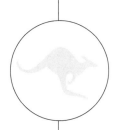

Just outside of Norseman, we set up camp on a patch of gravel that had been left behind from road surfacing. For the first time since New South Wales, we had a dry, mud-free camping area.

Stepping down from the van, I was overcome with a feeling of lonely isolation. It was almost as though we shouldn't be there. "It's as though we're the only ones on the planet," I told Bill. "How can that be when we're just outside a town of 4,000 people?"

It's a beautiful place, too," he said. "Look at the rolling green hills. This is what it was like when we started out from Sydney—wheat and dairy country. We're back to civilization," he smiled, trying to cheer me up.

I shrugged off the uneasy feeling. "Maybe it's because everyone we met on the Nullarbor was an immediate friend."

"We did meet some great people on the Nullarbor," Bill said, lifting down the kitchen awning from the roof rack. "But people here are friendly, too. Especially that shopkeeper when we arrived at the weekend closing hour. I had forgotten, again, that shops close from Saturday noon until Monday morning. We were lucky."

I laughed. "We did have to scurry around to find a store still open, didn't we? Yes, the shopkeeper was very nice." I lifted Jackie down to play with Pam and Tia while we unpacked.

Thirty minutes later, we had created a brand new, though temporary, "home site," complete with a friendly campfire's glow. "Now, doesn't that make you feel better?" Bill asked, admiring the scene.

"I'll feel better when we get settled," I sighed. "How about rounding up the kids. Dinner's almost ready."

We turned in for the night, cozy and warm. A few hours later, I woke up freezing. It was bitter cold. Our two blankets weren't enough. I whispered to Bill, who wasn't sleeping either, "I don't think the van's insulation is adequate for this climate. I had better check on Pam and Tia."

"Righto. I'll see how the boys are doing in the tent," Bill said.

Tia and Pam were warm enough in their sleeping bags, but Jackie started to fuss when Bill came back in. I put her in our bed and added her blanket to our two. "The boys are fine," Bill reported as we all snuggled together under three blankets. "It's warmer in the tent than it is in here."

The alarm rang at 5:30. "I don't know about you," I muttered to Bill, "but I'm going to stay in bed until the sun warms things up." Even after the sun rose, most of us shivered through breakfast. I was sitting in the van, wearing my jacket with hands curled around a hot cup of coffee, when Bill announced, "I'm going to wash the van from the rainwater sump nearby."

I couldn't believe my ears. Here I am freezing, and he's going out to slosh around in water? I called the boys. "How would you like to build another fire?" Without taking time to answer, they ran off in three directions to hunt for wood. In no time, we had a nice warm fire between the tent and the van.

While Bill washed the van outside, I did the best I could inside. "It would take a powerful vacuum cleaner to do a really good job," I mumbled to Tia who was helping me. Our new van had aged a year in just three weeks of travel. Everything—including us—had taken a terrific pounding coming across the Nullarbor.

It was still cold when we started out for the day. The laundry hadn't dried, and I was out of diapers. Before we left, I draped several from the seat backs to dry. We sat shivering in the van while Bill tied down the canvas on the roof rack. I couldn't help feeling akin to the pioneer women who had crossed America in covered wagons. I could imagine them shivering as their wagons bounced along and wondering, "Will we ever get to our destination?"

Even though it was cold, the paved road was a pleasure to drive on. We saw signs of flooding, and, in some places, water poured across the road. We had no choice but to proceed carefully, praying the van wouldn't stall or or get washed away.

Passing several small towns, sheep farms and grain fields, we stopped outside of Merredin for lunch. Sitting in a circle on camp stools, I quizzed the children. "Who knows how many miles 'til we get to Perth?"

"Not soon enough," Rusty ventured.

"Probably hundreds," Mickey frowned.

"I don't care as long as we get there soon," Skippy declared.

Perched on her daddy's lap, Pam piped up, "A hundred and fifty!"

"Daddy told her," Tia shouted. "I heard him."

"Time to go," Dad said, trying not to laugh. "If we're going to make Perth before dark, we had better get started." With that good news, everyone scampered back into the van.

We arrived in Perth at sunset. Bill stopped at the police station to ask if there were any caravan parks close to the city. "There's only one," he was told. "They don't allow tents, but they do have caravans for hire."

After a quick conference, we decided to rent one of the trailers. The park was not particularly clean, but it had good laundry facilities. Deciding to make the best of it, we unpacked and settled for the night. Tomorrow would determine the direction our new life would take.

We found Perth to be a beautiful city. It was young, new and well laid out, the pride of Western Australia. Our long-range plan was to get some experience with farming before we bought a farm. Bill's list of choices were: agricultural school, a farm job or construction job, in that order.

Bright and early the next morning, he started the rounds with high hopes. He didn't find a job the first day, but he came home with a heater for the caravan. It was wonderful! We were finally warm. For the next week, Bill was gone all day every day on his quest for a job. Rusty, Mickey and

Skippy, always the first to investigate our surroundings, made a great discovery. "Mom," Skippy first was home with the news, "just across the highway there's a park."

"It's right on the Swan River," Mickey added.

"Can we go fishing?" Rusty asked. They kept busy the rest of the day with worms and fishing poles. The girls and I occupied our time making the little trailer clean and homey.

Getting the girls to sleep at night was a major chore. Pam and Jackie were on the bottom bunk and Tia on the top. Now everybody knows you can't win with a combination like that. But we had no choice. They talked and giggled way past bedtime. The boys bunked in the van while Bill and I slept on a horribly uncomfortable breakfast-nook bed.

One morning after exploring, the boys rushed in all excited. "We met some kids who live right next to the park," Skippy announced.

"They traveled all over Australia, living in a big touring car," Rusty said. "Mr. Kiley told us the car is over thirty years old."

Mickey picked up Jackie. "Guess what?" he told her. "Mr. Kiley is a cook, a mechanic, a drover and an overseer. He does everything. And," he added, tickling her tummy, "Mrs. Kiley wants us to come over for tea tonight at 7:00."

"Our whole family?" I was surprised.

"Yes, can we go?" Skippy asked anxiously.

"That's wonderful! Please tell them we'll come." After they rushed off, I began to wonder. Tea at 7:00? I was familiar with the English custom of afternoon tea, but evening tea? Should I feed the family first? If I did, and tea turned out to be a meal, we might insult them by not doing it justice. When the boys came home, I sent them back to find one of their new friends to educate us. "Ask them what they mean by 'tea.'"

In a quick minute, they were back with a report. "Tea, or supper, depending on where you hail from, is the Australian dinner meal," Mickey recited.

That evening turned out to be one of the jewels of my life. Mr. Kiley, an Irishman, had visited the States during the second World War. He was a sailor on an English naval vessel at the time. Mrs. Kiley, an English woman, was a chatterbox with a heart of gold. After dinner, they entertained us with stories of their adventures. They had crisscrossed the Australian continent with three children in a vintage touring car. "We turned our hand to every job opportunity along the way," Mrs. Kiley said with a strong British accent.

"Yes, we've been everywhere," Mr. Kiley said quietly. Then, leveling a steady gaze at us, he declared, "Queensland. Go back East. It's the best and only place to live. You should go back there," he repeated. I mentally shuddered, remembering what it took to get from there to here. Smiling politely, I changed the subject.

Suddenly, the children appeared on the scene. It was showtime. Home movies? No. Television? No. Card games? No. For the next hour, Wendy, Maureen and Chris, the same ages as our boys, delighted us with poems and recitations they had made up or learned at school. Maureen, the oldest, stood demurely before us. She announced, "I shall recite, "Hiss, Hark, a Walk Through the Park" by C.J. Dennis, one of Australia's most famous poets." She began, acting out the parts as she spoke:

"Hist!... Hark!
The night is very dark,

And we've to go a mile or so
Across the Possum Park
Step... light;
Keeping to the right...."

The poem went on about scary things like the sudden hoot of an owl, croak of a frog and hiss of a cat. Her performance was delightful. We were impressed. These two girls and their brother had often missed attending regular school but were smart, poised and confident.

"They do correspondence school," Mrs. Kiley explained. "When we're working at a station, they talk to their teachers over two-way radios at a certain time each day. Sometimes, the teachers are miles away, but the system works well."

"That sounds like fun," Rusty said.

"Not if you get scolded over a two-way radio," Wendy frowned.

"School is never fun," Chris said, grabbing Skippy by the arm and running outside to play.

When it was close to bedtime, we thanked the Kileys for a delicious dinner and wonderful evening's entertainment. We walked home in a merry mood, chattering happily about our new friends.

A week later, Bill was offered a farm job in Geraldton, 300 miles north of Perth. Promising to keep in touch with the Kileys, we packed up and set out with high spirits. We had been told that the house they used for the farmhand's family did not have electric power. But we were optimistic—and green. We drove all day, happily planning all the things we were going to do on the farm.

"Can we have horses to ride?" Skippy asked.

"I think we should have some cows for milk," Rusty said. "I could take care of those."

"We could use the horses to round them up," Skippy suggested.

"You don't round up milk cows," Rusty said, rolling his eyes heavenward.

Tia offered to take care of the chickens. "We would have lots of eggs to make cookies and things."

We arrived in Geraldton at sundown. Bill reported at the boss's house. It was a lovely, modern, brick home high on a bluff overlooking the town. "He'll be out soon to show us the farm," Bill said when he came back. We sat in the van waiting. It seemed like forever. Finally, the boss came out, climbed into his truck and drove off. We followed.

During the last gray light of day, he took us through the worker's quarters. My stomach churned as we went from room to room. Bill and I had already discussed the possibility of the house being unsuitable for our family. "If it's necessary, I can suggest renting a place in town," he had told me. "The experience of working on a farm would be worth paying the extra money."

The boys were bubbling over with enthusiasm. It was a blow when I announced we would camp in our tent as usual instead of the house. All during dinner, they wanted to know what was wrong with the house. At this point, any house would have seemed wonderful to them.

After dinner, we decided to conduct them on a tour by lantern light. We went through the back door past the reeking, filthy WC. I didn't realize it at the time, but indoor plumbing was quite a luxury in these parts. It just needed to be flushed and cleaned.

We quickly passed on to one of the back rooms. "This is the combination egg-sorting room and laundry," I told them. It was piled high with dirt and debris. There was a wood-heated laundry copper and two set tubs but no washing machine.

I knew about coppers and set tubs. I could see myself stoking the fire under the copper and standing over those tubs, scrubbing away by the hour. We went on to the kitchen which contained a wood-burning stove of early vintage and a sink—no cabinets, no counters, no storage at all.

The living room and two bedrooms were both empty of furniture or closets. The bathroom was in a sorry state. We finished out on the front porch where broken windows and disuse were equally evident. Still, the charm of a "house" prevailed for the boys until, on the way back through, a door fell down on Pam's head. Apparently, the door had been taken off it's hinges and leaned against the wall. "She's all right," I assured the boys who were suddenly quiet. "Dad caught the door just in time." Promises of house hunting in town the next morning soothed everyone. With very high hopes, we went to bed.

The next day, when Bill suggested we rent a house in town, the station owner regretfully explained he needed a farmhand who would live on the property. Also, the farm worker's wife was expected to be available to help in the "big house."

We agonized over the decision. It would be difficult to live in a house that was apt to fall down around us. It would be even more difficult to cope with no electricity. "Practically everything we own is electrical," I told Bill. "And how would I ever be able to take care of six children *and* the big house?"

"You're right," he said carefully. "That would be expecting an awful lot from you. Plus, we would have to buy a lot of furniture."

There was an other alternative that kept creeping into our thoughts: the seed that had been planted in our minds by Mr. Kiley. "Go back East to Queensland," he had said. I remembered the lonely feeling of not belonging when we arrived in Western Australia. Was that a premonition?

We thought of Uncle Tom who was such a good friend aboard ship. He was back East—in Queensland. After a great deal of prayer, and long, shuddering thoughts of another trek across the Nullarbor, we finally decided we could make a better start in Queensland.

Chapter Fifteen

Reverse Procedure

"We need to let the Kileys know," Bill said when we reached Perth. "We might as well stop on our way to the campground. The Kileys were surprised to see us back so soon and invited us in for a cup of tea. In the middle of our tale about Geraldton, the children, who had been playing outside, came rushing in. "They're going to Queensland," Wendy shouted.

"I want them to stay here," Chris pouted at the thought of losing his new chums. Mr. and Mrs. Kiley were delighted with our decision. They insisted we stay with them while we prepared for the return trip. Two days later, we were ready to say goodbye to new friends who seemed like old friends. With much encouragement from the whole family, we set out for Queensland.

The trip across as "sun downers" had taken almost three weeks. Ten days later we were headed back, not as tourists, but as experienced travelers. We were determined to make short work of what lay ahead.

The roads were dryer and some stretches had been graded. The dust was still thick but not unbearable. The rain had stopped in most areas, although we heard on the radio that one town was flooded the day after we passed. The weather was cold and often bitter. "We're part of history in the making again," Bill reported, after a stop for petrol. "This is the coldest winter on record."

"I can agree to that," I said, turning up the heat to compensate for the cold wind that followed him into the van. "I hope the next history-making event will be 'good' news for a change."

Bill nodded and proposed a plan. "Instead of setting up camp at sundown, why don't we make up beds in the van during our dinner stop. Then the children can sleep while we drive a few extra hours."

As a team, Bill and I became experts at zipping on the awning, setting up the tent, unrolling sleeping bags, shifting the children into them and unpacking the roof rack. Our record night was fifteen minutes from the time we stopped until we had water boiling for coffee.

From New South Wales on, we paused briefly in towns of any size to check on farm work. Nothing was available. It was wet and it was winter. Farming was at a standstill. We had traveled out during the worst rainy season in thirty years and back during the coldest winter on record. Now, we were hearing about the worst year for farm jobs. "I guess that's the next record you were wondering about," Bill said with a frown.

"You're right, that's the bad news. But the good news, during this history-making year, is that the Moores have survived it all."

Undaunted, we arrived in Queensland. As soon as we crossed the state line, we felt at home. It seemed God had something special for us in this kangaroo country. We all agreed the trip back East was worth the effort.

Right after we entered the state, we saw our first group of wild emus. The ones we had seen in cages hadn't prepared us for the real thing. We stopped to watch. The small flock was stepping along at a regal pace, but suddenly they were off with the speed of race horses. "Wow, did you see that!" Bill exclaimed. The children all started laughing and talking at once. The emus had been a wonderful show after the long dusty days across the outback.

Rusty, craning his neck to watch a red eagle cruising in circles above us, murmured softly, "I like Queensland."

"I do, too," Mickey echoed, "but I miss the Kileys. They were nice."

"Yes," I agreed, "let's hope we see them again someday."

Suddenly, Skippy shouted, "Hey look, a kangaroo!"

Pam climbed up beside Tia to look out the window. Mickey held up Jackie. "See, see the kangaroo," he pointed. Bill stopped by the roadside. We watched the kangaroo hop toward a small herd. The herd stood motionless, no doubt wondering if we were a threat. "Look at the ones sitting on their tails," Rusty said excitedly. Finally, realizing that we were harmless, the herd bounded on its way without a backward glance.

"Wow," I said in awe. "I never dreamed I'd see a real kangaroo sitting on it's tail. I'm going to like Queensland."

Tia put her arm around Pam's shoulder. "I like Queensland, too," she said, giving her a hug. Pam giggled, not quite sure what a "Queensland" was.

"I'm glad you all like Queensland," Bill said over his shoulder, "because we'll be in Brisbane by dinner time."

"Hurrah," the kids shouted.

Brisbane, the capital of Queensland, was a large sprawling city that had grown up helter skelter. We were told people found their way through the maze of streets by following the trolley tracks. At the police station, we were directed to a campground just outside of the city. We set up camp and settled down. The next day, Bill and I began our hunt for a place to rent. "Do you have children?" was the first question asked.

"Yes, we have six."

"Sorry."

Or perhaps it went like this: "Do you have a reference from your last landlord?"

"No, we just arrived here from the States."

"Sorry."

"What shall we do?" I asked Bill. "We can't live in the campground for ever." As we poured over the 'For Rent' ads, I spotted one that said, "For rent with option to buy."

"Let's try that," I suggested. "We don't have to buy it, but at least we'll have a place to live until we decide what to do."

Bill went off to see the house. I paced nervously, straining to hear the van the minute it entered the campground. When he came in, I could tell by the expression on his face that he had good news. "Do you want to go take look?" he asked. "I told the agent you would like to see it."

"Yes!" I said. "Rusty is not far off. I'll call him to watch the others." Within minutes, the children were settled and we were off.

The house was in Clayfield, a suburb on the main road to Brisbane. Like most Australian houses, it was built up on stilts for coolness and protection from white ants. The large cemented area underneath was enclosed with lattice work. There was room enough for a car, a thousand-gallon water-storage tank and a laundry. The laundry area had a washing machine and gas-heated copper. A flush toilet was in a separate little WC on the side. The rest of the bathroom was upstairs—very confusing when you're accustomed to finding the "bathroom" all in one place.

The agent guided us up outside stairs to the kitchen. It had a sink, gas stove and pantry but no cupboards. Seeing my puzzled expression, the agent explained, "Australians furnish their own kitchen units." He went on to describe the type of kitchen cabinets popular in America during the '30s and '40s.

We walked through a good-sized dining room and three bedrooms. The large living room was in the front of the house with an enclosed porch that overlooked the street. "This is available with an option to buy," he told us. We looked at each other and nodded.

"We'll take it." Bill said. I smiled. I felt sure we wouldn't be there for long. This was suburb living. We wanted more space for the kids to roam, but this would be fine for now. We arranged to move in that afternoon.

Back at the campground, the children were elated by the news. "Is it a big house?" Mickey wanted to know.

"Is there room for ponies?" Rusty asked.

Tia, who had been sharing a bunk with one of the girls, looked up at me earnestly and asked, "Can I have my own bed?"

"It's big enough," I answered Mickey. "But ponies..." I looked at Rusty, "not yet. Tia, right now there are only two beds in the whole place, and you can sleep on one of them. The rest of us will use cushions from the van and sleeping bags. As soon as we can, we'll shop for beds."

When we returned to the house, a closer look revealed that the house had been unoccupied for a very long time. There was a thick layer of dust everywhere. I spread out tarps and newspapers to put our things on while Bill brought up the luggage.

The next day, I went to a little shop down the street to buy a broom, dustpan and cleaning supplies. With frustrated thoughts of my vacuum cleaner in storage, I swept up countless dustpans full of dust from the carpets. "It's all right," I calmed myself, "we won't be here for long."

After Bill unpacked and cleaned the van, he poked his head in the door. "I'm going to find a pay phone," he said. "I want to let Tom know we're here in Queensland." Tom's sugar plantation was in Mackay, 600 miles north of us.

"What did Tom say?" I asked when he came back.

"The person who answered told me Tom wasn't there."

"Oh, that's too bad. Did you leave a message?"

"No."

"Why not?"

"Because Tom's in Brisbane on business. When I told them who I was, they gave me his Brisbane phone number."

"That's amazing! Tom Barfield in Brisbane just when we arrive from Perth. Are you going to call him?"

Bill is a twenty-questions person. I waited for his next bit of information. "I did. He and his wife are visiting friends."

"Will they be in Brisbane long?"

"I don't know, but I invited them over for tea tomorrow afternoon." He announced this news with a big grin, certain I'd be thrilled.

Without answering, I looked around the house in dismay. We had a dining table and chairs but no furniture in the living room. The strings hanging from the bottom of the aged lace curtains made me wonder if the previous owner had owned a cat. I sighed and looked steadily at Bill. "We have a lot of work to do before tomorrow—starting right now."

I turned to Tia. "Get my little scissors, and I'll show you how to trim the strings on the curtains. Bill, if you and Rusty put the trunks in the living room, we can put the cushions from the van on them to make two little sofas. Mickey, find the menus from the ship with the water-color paintings on the front. They'll look nice on the walls. Skippy, go down to one of the shops and ask for an empty carton. We can cover it with something to make a coffee table. Pam, I saw some flowers downstairs. You and Jackie can pick them, but," I looked at them sternly, "remember, you mustn't go out of the yard." Everyone bustled around making the house presentable. We did the best we could with what we had. When we finished, it looked cozy and livable. The next morning, at the little neighborhood store, I bought cups, saucers and a tea pot. On the way home, I picked up pastries from the bake shop. We were ready to entertain.

The children were thrilled when Tom arrived. Jackie ran over to be picked up. Pam was right behind her. He held them both while he introduced Margaret, his wife. We were delighted to meet her. After the excitement subsided, Tom said, "Tell us about your trip."

Over tea and pastries we entertained them with our adventures. Rusty told Tom about fishing. "I didn't catch much," he said. "I guess I had the wrong kind of bait for Australian fish."

Tom, who liked to fish, gave him a tip for a good catch. "Roll up bread into small balls," he suggested, "and bait your hook with them."

Mickey told them about the bandicoots we saw outside Wirulla. "I tried to catch one, but they disappeared into their burrow so fast."

"We saw emus at one campground," Skippy reported. "I wanted to ride one, but Mom said it was not allowed."

Tom couldn't help smiling, "That would have been quite a show," he chuckled.

Tia was not to be left out. "We saw lots of kangaroos. One of them had a little joey in her pocket. He was so cute."

"When I was a young girl," Margaret told her, "I had a little joey. He had gotten lost from his mother. I fed him with a baby bottle until he got big enough to hop away."

"Wow," Tia said, wide-eyed. "Maybe I can find one to play with." At this point, I suggested the children go outside for awhile. I poured fresh cups of tea and we settled down for a time of adult conversation.

"I want to thank you for calling," Tom said. "I couldn't have been more surprised. And to think we were visiting right here in Brisbane. I'm glad you decided on Queensland." He looked at Bill, "Have you made any plans yet?"

"I haven't really had time," Bill explained. "My first plan was to attend an Agriculture School before buying a farm. They didn't have one in Perth, and I haven't found one here. Then we spent a lot of time looking a place to live. It's quite a trick trying to rent a house in Brisbane when you have a family."

"I know," Tom was sympathetic. "Landlords are picky. Not everyone has children who behave as well as yours."

When he was getting ready to leave, Tom asked if there was anything he could do for us. He tactfully wondered if we needed financial assistance. Bill thanked him and assured him we had made an allowances in case he didn't get a job right away. We called the children back inside to bid them goodbye. "You must come Mackay to see us some time soon," Margaret insisted. We assured her we would. Standing on the steps, waving goodbye to these special friends, I couldn't help blinking back a few tears.

Inside, we collected the tea things to take to the kitchen. "It's be hard to get homesick when everyone we meet is so friendly," I sighed. "If Tom and Margaret are a sample of Queenslanders, I think we've come to the right place."

Bill nodded as he reached for a towel to wipe while I washed. "And the Queensland climate reminds me of California," he said. "Besides, we can see an American movie at the nearest theater and turn on the radio for American hit tunes and shows...."

"And," I added, "we can buy American products—or reasonable facsimiles—in American-type department stores."

"The only difficult thing," Bill said, stacking the dishes, "is getting adjusted to the Holy Sabbath again. It still surprises me when everything closes from Saturday noon until Monday morning."

"It does take a bit of getting used to," I agreed, "but, frankly, I think it's a great idea!"

Chapter Sixteen

Settling In

It didn't take long for the boys to become friends with all the shopkeepers on our side of the highway. They made the rounds daily, often putting Jackie in her stroller and taking the girls with them. I suspected they shared a lot of family news along the way. How else would the baker know we liked whole-wheat bread? He made it a point to save us a loaf each day.

The "bakery lady" treated them to sweets and often sent little cakes home for Mom and Dad. The barber gave tips on fishing to Rusty. The grocery owner showed Mickey all the latest gadgets. Skippy's favorite spot was the hardware store with all the hunting equipment.

One morning, I suggested to Rusty, "Now that we're settled, why don't you ask your shopkeeper friends about schools in this area."

After making his morning rounds, he came home with good news. "The bakery lady said there is a private school just up the road. We could walk there, she said. That's better than having to take a bus," he grinned. We discovered that all Australian school children, public and private, wore uniforms. This school was no exception. We dutifully enrolled the children and shopped for the necessary outfits. The boys' uniform was a white shirt, necktie (in school colors), short dress pants, knee socks and a wide-brim felt hat. Dressed for school, they looked very Australian.

Although Tia wouldn't be old enough for school until the new year began in January, I could picture her in her uniform. She would be wearing a white blouse, the school necktie, a navy tunic (that's Australian for jumper) and wide-brim straw hat. She would also have knee socks and the same type of sturdy, black shoes the boys wore. As I thought about her going off to school with her brothers, I wanted to cry. My dainty little girl wearing a necktie and boy's shoes!

The boys also had backpacks called book bags. They were rigid containers with shoulder straps and rounded corners that held all their books. On Fridays, they carried sports clothes. "Everyone plays sports on Friday," Mickey told me. "You can come some day when we have our special Sports Day Program." To them, this new school system was a great adventure.

With the children settled, Bill began looking for a job. During his early Navy career with the Sea Bees, he had learned to operate heavy equipment. "It's a trade that always comes in handy," he often remarked. And it did. He soon found a job as a crane operator with the Moreton Light and Tug Company.

Settling In

On weekends, we went exploring. Our time on the road had made us excellent campers, ready to go in a matter of minutes. There was so much to see, and with our van, we could park anywhere.

Rusty's barber friend told him, "The Condimine: it's the best place for good fishing. Fair dinkum, you can't beat it for a good catch."

"Can we go to Dalby?" Rusty asked when he came home.

"Where's Dalby and what for?" I wanted to know.

He had done his homework well. "It's 180 miles west and right on the Condimine River. I want to go fishing there."

"I'll ask your dad," I promised. "We've never been out that way."

On our next outing, we spent Saturday camped by the lovely tree-lined Condimine River. As soon as we set up camp, Rusty had his fishing gear out. He was full of excitement about trying his new fishing techniques. His friend was right. An afternoon of fishing provided a nice catch for dinner.

Curious three-year-old Pam wasn't quite as lucky. She strayed too close to the steep bank, lost her balance and slipped into the river. We heard a splash and rushed to investigate. It was Skippy who had made the splash. Always quick in a crisis, he had jumped in to rescue her. By the time we got there, he was climbing the bank, holding his sister like a trophy. She was coughing, sputtering and dripping wet—but safe. I quickly wrapped her in a towel and took her to the van for some cuddling and dry clothes. Clean, dry, cautious but undaunted, she was soon ready to go back outside. That evening, we celebrated both catches—Rusty's fish and Skippy's Pam.

Sunday after church, we moved on to Bradshaw Lake. "This is a busy resort in the summertime," Bill noted from a brochure. "But it looks as though only a few water skiers are braving the cold weather."

After the skiers left, a flock of huge black swans took over the lake. "Oh, look at those!" I said, amazed. "I have never seen black swans before."

"That's because black swans are found only in Australia," Bill informed me from his fund of information.

"You should see their wing span!" Rusty cried. "Come on," he called to the others. "Let's show Mom how wide their wings spread when they fly." They all charged down to the water yelling like Indians on the war path. The swans were not a bit impressed. They flapped their wings a little and settled down again.

"Never mind," I told Bill. "It's more of a thrill to watch our little band—from toddler to big brother—joining together to please Mom." It was a wonderful weekend, a memory to treasure.

Back in Brisbane, Bill's search for a place to rent came to a dead end. After a morning of hunting, he came home to report, "No one wants to rent to people with children." We talked about the problem. "I was hoping we could find a house like this somewhere," Bill said.

Suddenly, I had a brilliant idea. "Why don't we buy this house? It can be an investment until we find a farm."

"You wouldn't mind?" Bill asked in surprise.

"No, I don't know why I didn't think of it before." Immediately, I began to see the possibilities! I turned to Bill, getting excited with the prospect. "This house is well built, strong and sturdy. Lots of scrubbing and a fair amount of paint inside and out would make it quite presentable."

"A coat of paint would definitely improve its value," Bill agreed.

"Righto. It's time to settle, at least for awhile," I said.

We shopped for paint, brushes, rollers and all the odds and ends needed to make a beginning. We were ready to start when I realized the rooms were ten-feet high. "We don't have a ladder," I moaned. "How can we reach the top of the walls or paint ceilings?"

Bill thought for a second. "I'll be right back," he said. In a few minutes, he rattled through the door with the spare metal garbage can from downstairs. "We can stand on this," he proclaimed, satisfied that he had solved the problem. "The lid is solid, and it's four feet high. That should do it." And it did. It was fine as long as he was was the one painting; he was six inches taller than I.

But it was a very different story when I painted while he was at work. Balancing the brush in one hand and a paint can in the other, I would gingerly climb up on a chair and step onto the garbage can lid. As long as I was near a wall, I could put my hand out to steady myself. But when it was time to do the ceiling, in the middle of the room, it was more like a circus, high-wire act. Climbing up and down with nothing to hang on to was a precarious business. I had visions of being startled by something and landing on the floor in a paint-splattered heap.

One afternoon, Bill came home early and caught me doing my high-wire act. "Why didn't you tell me?" he scolded. "Don't paint any more until I get a step ladder."

The step ladder was a great improvement. The ceilings in the main bedroom and living room were ornamental plaster with bas-relief flowers and scrolls. Old paint, hanging in shreds, had to be scraped off before we could put on a new coat. It took a stiff brush and weeks to clean all the little lines and grooves of that scroll work.

With a lot of perseverance, the inside was beautifully finished by the time the weather was warm enough for us to paint the outside. Bill bought an extension ladder, and we divided the work. "Would you like me to paint the siding while you paint the windows?" he asked.

"Sure," I said. Sounded like a good deal to me; it was a big house. Then I counted the French windows. There were over a dozen plus the French doors. "I think I've been had," I muttered, totaling all the small window panes.

Clinging to a two-story ladder, painting fiddley wood strips between small panes of glass was not my idea of a tranquil pastime. But then, of course, Bill had a lot more area to paint than I did. When we finished, the house looked brand new and very New England—gleaming white with dark-green trim. It reminded us of Maine where we grew up.

In September, the Sunday paper carried a three-page spread about some island farms out in Moreton Bay. The word "island" was the magic key. Bill had often talked about the wonderful islands off the coast of Maine. "Would you like to go look at these islands?" he asked. "There's a ferry that leaves in the morning and comes back in the afternoon."

"I have so much to do here," I hedged. "Why don't you make it a day's outing? You can tell me all about the islands when you get back."

His face fell; he doesn't like to travel alone. But he was still determined. "How about taking Tia?" he asked.

"Fine," I said. "A five-year-old can be a lot of company." Then, as an afterthought, I added, "Why don't you take Pam, too." Pam's sense of curiosity and adventure was very strong. I realized it would be easier to include her than to explain why she couldn't go.

They left early in the morning with a basket loaded with supplies. I had packed bathing suits in case the islanders happened to be frolicking in the water surrounding them, jackets in case the journey across the windswept waves became chilly, a washcloth, bib and change of clothes for Pam who was still young for an all-day trip, and, of course, lunch.

After they left, I picked up the newspaper article. "A Lovely Corner of the Bay" was the title. I read on: "…an unexploited haven of tranquility, only ninety minutes by boat and bus from Brisbane, but a world apart in atmosphere. This thriving farming community is as peaceful as it was at the turn of the century." The article went on to say that the four islands, Russell, Karragarra, Lamb and Macleay, just six miles offshore, had a total population of 275 and that everyone knew everyone else's business. "Well, we'll see," I muttered to myself.

Chapter Seventeen

A Special Visit

"WHERE'S DAD?" SKIPPY, ARRIVING home from school, stood in the doorway expectantly. "Did he like the islands?"

"Yeah," Mickey pushed past him to pick up Jackie. "Are we going to move?"

"Is there room for ponies?" Rusty asked, joining the other two.

"Simmer down," I cautioned. "Dad only went for an outing. Let's get dinner ready. He should be home soon. Rusty, you peel the potatoes. Skippy, since Tia isn't here, you set the table. I've baked your favorite meat loaf and only need to finish the mashed potatoes and vegetables. Dad should be home by then."

"What do you want me to do?" Mickey asked.

"Would you entertain Jackie in the living room. This kitchen is small, and I don't want her to get in the way. She's been so lonely today. It's the first time Tia and Pam haven't been here for her to play with."

With dinner almost ready, I wondered what else I could do to keep the boys from becoming fidgety. Just then, Mickey burst into the kitchen. Since the living room was in the the front of the house, he had heard the van the moment it turned into the driveway. "Dad's here!" he yelled, dashing out the door and down the steps with Jackie in his arms.

I heard a babble of questions down below followed by Bill's quiet voice. "I'll tell you all about it at dinner time. Help carry things upstairs, and we'll go eat."

"I'll take Jackie," Tia said, reaching for her little sister.

"I'll take Pam," Mickey said, scooping her up and perching her on his shoulders. Bill and the other boys unloaded the van and followed them upstairs.

Standing at the top of the steps, I was as curious as the boys were to hear the news. I wished I could stop everything to ask a dozen questions. The boys wanted to know if we were moving to the islands. I wanted to know that we were not. "It was a wonderful trip," Bill said after we settled at the table and he had blessed the food.

"We went on a boat," Pam beamed, missing the target with her spoon.

"Righto," Bill paused, reaching over to wipe the potato off her chin. "We stopped at three islands before we got to Russell. Karragara was the smallest, only a mile long and not quite a mile wide." He glanced at the boys. "That's about the distance you walk to school."

"I wouldn't want to live there," Skippy said. "I might ride my bike right off the end."

"You don't even have a bike," Rusty corrected.

A Special Visit

"I will when we get our shipment from the States."

"What about the other islands?" I asked to bring the story back on track.

"The next one, Macleay, was twice as big. Lamb Island was small but Russell was the biggest—three miles by five miles."

"That's not very big," I said.

"It doesn't seem that way, but remember Chincoteague Island?"

"Of course. It's off the coast of Virginia. We lived there while we were waiting for base housing. It was just before Rusty was born, and we got there by a bridge—not by a boat. Why do you ask?"

"Chincoteague wasn't quite as big as Russell Island."

"Really! Do many people live there?"

"Actually, 120 people live on the island. Most of them are farmers. When we got there, they were loading produce that they had brought down to the jetty from their farms."

Mickey nodded. "My teacher told us that lots of fruit and vegetables come from the islands. She said a big truck goes over on a barge. The farmers load their things on the truck. Then the big truck drives right onto the barge to bring everything back to Brisbane to sell."

"That's right," his dad agreed.

"We got bananas!" Tia said, waving her fork in the air. "The farmer gave them to us. Daddy saved them for after dinner."

"Righto," Bill smiled. "Everyone was very friendly. A fellow named Ron Pointon treated us to bananas. Another 'bloke' (as the Aussies say) named Bill Martin gave us a ride around the island...."

"We saw a school," Tia interrupted. "The kids were having a picnic under the school...."

"Don't interrupt," Dad admonished. He quieted her with a look and continued with his story. "It was a two-room schoolhouse built up on stilts like our house. There were tables underneath so the children could eat in the shade. Mr. Martin told me that children from the other islands came over to school on the ferry boat."

"Were there any horses?" Rusty asked.

"I didn't see any. But a farmer at the jetty said that just a few years ago, everyone had horses as their only means of transportation. They used them to work their crops and to carry produce down to the barge. He said that only one farmer does that now. Everyone else uses tractors and trucks."

"Did you see any kangaroos?" Skippy wanted to know.

"No, there aren't any on the island. But the shopkeeper told me there are wallabies."

"Wow, wallabies!" Rusty said. "I'd love to see those pint-sized kangaroos."

Mickey brightened at the mention of a shopkeeper. "Is the store very big? What do they sell?"

"I saw sugar, flour, canned goods and things like that."

"Do they sell candy?" Skippy asked.

Pam threw back her head and giggled. "Yes, they do. Daddy bought us some!"

Bill turned to me with a questioning look, wondering what I thought about all this. "I think you would like it over there," he offered. "We could go over on one of my days off."

"That's a possibility," I said, not wanting to make a commitment. I stood up. "Who wants brownies and ice cream for dessert?"

A Special Visit

"We do!" they shouted in chorus. Talk of the islands faded in favor of brownies and ice cream and the day's school events.

Soon after that, our temporary shipment arrived from the States. Most of it was housekeeping necessities and very welcomed. We busied ourselves making more adjustments, especially with the school year coming to a close. In Australia, the school year ends in November for summer vacation and begins again in January. The children had only been attending since August and weren't excited about another change.

It was time to think about Christmas. What would we do for the holidays? All of our Christmas things were in storage in the States, and we were far away from our families. "This is going to be a challenge," I whispered in prayer.

As if on cue, Mickey came in with the mail. "We've got a letter from the Barfields," he said excitedly. "Can you open it right now?"

I slid open the envelope with a kitchen knife and lifted out the letter. I quickly scanned it: "Hope you are all well..." my eyes slid down the page. "...would it be possible for you to visit us for Christmas?" I gasped. Talk about answered prayer!

"What is it?" Mickey asked, wide-eyed.

"They want us to go up there for Christmas!"

"Can we? Can we? Oh Mom, can we?"

"I don't know, Mickey. We'll talk about it when Dad gets home."

I waited patiently for Bill to take off his heavy work shoes downstairs and unload his lunch box on the cupboard before I presented the letter. He read it through and looked up. "What a wonderful, generous thing for them to do!" he said in awe. "It will be like having Christmas with family."

The children were thrilled. The islands were forgotten. Mackay was the only topic of the day with countless questions. "How far is it?"

"Six hundred miles."

"What's it like?"

Rusty answered that one. "It's sugar-cane country between the ocean and the Clarke Mountain Range. I learned that at school."

"How many kids do they have?"

"Four. Michael, the oldest, is about Skippy's age, then there is Philip, Francis and Teresa who is four years old." To give them something to do besides ask questions, I suggested we start making plans. "Why don't you decide what you want take with you in your travel bags."

"I know what I'm going to take," Pam said. "I'm going to take my doll to show Teresa. She's the same age as me."

"Are we going to camp on the way?" Skippy asked. "Cause, if we do, can we take hotdogs to cook over the campfire?"

"Mmm," I said, tickling his neck. "I think it must be time for dinner."

Bill's job gave him two weeks off for Christmas vacation. With great anticipation, we loaded the van and set out on the road again. We drove along the coastal highway beside the beautiful blue waters of the Pacific Ocean. At times, we could see beaches dotted with palm trees and teeming with surfers.

"Dad," Rusty asked, leaning over the seat back, "did you see those surfers? Could we stop at a beach?"

A Special Visit

Skippy's sharp ears picked up the plea. "Can we? I want to go swimming."

Tia rubbed her cheek against mine. "Mom, can we?" she coaxed.

It was almost lunchtime. I knew they were ready for a break. "What do you think, Hon?"

"We'll be in Bundaberg in about twenty minutes. It should have a nice beach with a picnic area. Has everyone got their bathing suits?"

"Yes!" they all shouted at once.

"All right. You can begin looking for a sign to a beach, and we'll check it out."

Suddenly, it was very quiet. They were all concentrating on being the first to find a sign. Jackie was the exception. "Can I have a cracker?"

"We're going to eat in a little while," I assured her.

"Here we are," Bill surprised us all as he turned off the highway.

"Oh Daddy! You knew all along!" Tia scolded.

"Well, I did read the map," he admitted.

We found a lovely, shaded picnic area, donned our suits and headed for the water. Bill and the boys chased the surf while the girls and I splashed around in the shallows until Jackie said, once more, "Can I have a cracker?"

Picking her up, I called to the others. "Lunch time! Okay Jackie, let's go find some real food." By the time we finished eating, our suits were reasonably dry. We changed in the van, said goodbye to the beach and headed for our next stop.

"We'll camp at Rockhampton," Bill said. "It's the largest city in this area. I'm sure we can find a campground where we'll be able to swim once more before we call it a day."

"Goody, goody," Tia said. "We can play in the water again," she told Jackie.

"Did you bring the hotdogs?" Skippy looked at me hopefully. I assured him that the hotdogs were in the cooler. We settled down to enjoy the beautiful mountains and lush forests. The afternoon sped by as we spotted kangaroos and emus. Sometimes, we saw strange birds we didn't have names for. By late afternoon, we reached Rockhampton. Climbing out of the van, we set up camp by the ocean to repeat our lunchtime frolic.

Later, we sat around the campfire roasting hotdogs on sticks and reminiscing. "I'm sure glad we met Uncle Tom on the boat coming over." Skippy said, gently tapping his hotdog to see if it was done.

"He's not really our uncle," Rusty mumbled with his mouth full of potato chips.

"I know that," Tia bristled, "but he wants us to call him 'uncle' just the same. That's the way Australians do it."

"I'm glad," Mickey said, "because if it wasn't for Uncle Tom, we wouldn't be in Queensland, sitting on a beach and roasting hotdogs. Can I have another one, Mom?"

Chapter Eighteen

An Australian Christmas

THE NEXT DAY WE DROVE THROUGH beautiful mountains and on to sugar-cane country. Mickey was first to spot the fire. "Wow, look at the smoke!" he pointed. "The whole field is on fire! We need to get out of here!"

"They're just burning the sugar cane," his dad said calmly.

"Why?"

"They fire it to burn away the leaves and undergrowth. It makes it easier to cut. When I was in Hawaii in 1946, I saw cane fires burning all around our base. Had me worried at first until someone explained what was going on. The fire only burns the leaf but not the stalk where the sugar is."

"Dad," Rusty said, "why do people put their hands on their windshields when we go by?"

"That's because of the rocks the tires spin up. They call this road "the glass highway." It's because the stones shatter so many windshields. Putting their hands on the windshield helps to stop the vibration. If a stone should fly up, it keeps the glass from shattering. I've been seeing pieces of glass all along the road… hey this is our turnoff."

Bill veered to the left on to a country road. Fifteen minutes later, we turned into Uncle Tom's driveway. Climbing out of the van, we were greeted by a brown and white dog that came bounding out of the house. It was followed by Tom with Michael, Philip, Francis and Teresa. We had talked so much about them, the children felt they were meeting old friends not strangers. They headed toward the house chatting with each other. Tom explained that Margaret was in town and would be home soon.

Mickey rushed over to us. "Mom! Michael says they have a pool. Can we go swimming?"

I looked at Tom, who nodded yes. "Whoa," Bill held up his hand. "Let's unload the van first." Excitedly, everyone carried something into the house. Tom showed us where to put our bags. In a very short time, we were all relaxing by the pool, children in the water and adults on lounge chairs. Pam and Jackie were playing dolls with Teresa on the grass.

"How was your trip up?" Tom asked after the usual "Mom-Dad-look-at-me!" coming from the pool performers.

"Wonderful. The roads weren't bad, and our windshield is still intact," Bill reported, looking at things from a driver's point of view.

I continued the story, describing our beach stops at Bundaberg and Rockhampton. "Living in Clayfield, we don't get to the beach very much. The kids love the water as you can see."

"Before you leave," Tom said, "we'll take you to a beach where you can see the Barrier Reef islands in the distance. The Whitsunday Passage has some of the best coastal scenery in Australia. The reef is regarded by scientists as one of the marine wonders of the world. And there's some of the best fishing," he added with a grin.

The word "fishing" drew Rusty to the edge of the pool. "Could we fish there?" he asked, climbing out.

"I know a better place to fish," Tom said. "We're going to take the boat to the lake tomorrow for a picnic. You'll be able to swim, fish and water ski."

"Wow!" exclaimed Rusty. "Can I tell the others?"

"Why don't we wait until morning," Tom suggested. Just then, Margaret waved at us from the window. We went over to say hello.

"The children were playing so well, I didn't want to disturb them," she explained. "I'm going to start supper now. It won't take long."

Tom turned to Rusty. "Your dad wants to see the giant-size machines we use for planting and harvesting cane. If you round everyone up and get them dried off, I'll bring the truck around. We'll take a tour of the farm."

"Righto!" Rusty said, starting off.

"Thanks," Margaret smiled at Tom. "That will give me time to get dinner ready."

"Could I help?" I offered.

"Wonderful," she said. "We'll have time for a chat without the usual 'mommy' interruptions."

Dinner was on the table when everyone arrived from the

tour. They were bubbling with exciting tales of "giant" machines. After dinner, the kids played outside while we sat on the porch and talked. "What's this I hear about your moving to an island?" Margaret asked.

"Oh, that... Bill went over to see the islands in Morton Bay. He has always wanted to live on an island. I'm not so sure that I do. We lived on Chincoteague Island just off the coast of Virginia when we were first married. It was little, but it had a bridge to the mainland. Later, we lived on the island of Guam in the Pacific, but that was pretty big. It had everything we needed. And of course, we lived on the island of Honshu in Japan. That was so big, it didn't seem like an island. But the bay islands are small. Everything depends on boat travel. There is no doctor, no hospital, only one little store and no high school."

"The high school is our main problem," Bill added. "The island teens go by boat, but we're not sure what kind of education they get."

"Had you considered boarding school?" Tom asked. "Most Australian eighth-graders go to boarding schools. They have very high standards. In a few years, we'll enroll Michael in one that's not far from you. We're keen on his getting a good start."

I glanced at Bill. *Will this make the islands more attractive to him*, I wondered. I decided to change the subject. I turned to Margaret, "On the way up, we saw some cane fields burning. The kids were amazed. They would love to know more about sugar processing. It would be fun to take some first-hand information back to share at school."

"Why don't we show them the mill and dock at Hay Point on the way to the lake?" Margaret suggested, looking at Tom.

We started out early the next morning with ten excited children. Most of them were in the van. Tom led in his truck, towing the boat. When he stopped at the sugar mill, everyone piled out to see sugar in the making. "Sugar is just giant-sized grass," Uncle Tom explained. "It takes over a year to grow eight feet or more before it can be cut. We cut it and send it to the mill on that train over there."

"That's just a baby train," Tia said, looking at the scaled-down engine running on narrow-gauge tracks. "It's cute."

"It's certainly smaller than American trains," Tom agreed. "We'll have a quick look at the cane being shredded and crushed. After that, they put it through rollers to squeeze out the juice.

"Do we get to taste it?" Mickey asked.

"It wouldn't be very sweet," Tom explained, "It has to be boiled until it crystallizes into sugar. Queensland cane has a higher sugar content than any other country, " he said proudly. Lots of questions later, we left the factory and drove on to the Hay Point harbor.

"Wow! Look at that!" Skippy exclaimed. "They're pushing sand around with bulldozers. There are mountains of it on those cement slabs."

"I bet that's sugar," Rusty guessed.

"Too right," Tom said, climbing out of the truck. "They're getting it into position to be loaded onto the ships out there in the harbor. It's brown now, but it'll be refined into white sugar. Some of it will go to the United Kingdom, Japan, Canada and the United States."

"Gosh," Mickey said, "we may have been eating Australian sugar on our cereal even before we came here."

"Who's ready to go swimming?" Margaret laughed. With that, everyone scampered back into the vehicles, ready to picnic and swim and ski.

At the lake, water skiing was first on the list. Bill and the boys had never done it before. "Would you like to go first?" Tom asked Bill.

"Sure. What am I supposed to do?"

"Put on the skis, and crouch down in the shallow water. When the line gets taut, I'll speed up. As you start to move, gradually stand up and balance yourself." Bill waited until Tom started the boat. He followed directions to the letter and was up and sailing. All of a sudden, he flipped head over heels.

"What happened?" I asked Margaret.

"He didn't realize the boat was turning. It's all right, he's up again."

One by one, the boys took their turns. After a little floundering, Rusty and Mickey zoomed off. Skippy got up on the skis as though he had been born for the sport. "Now it's your turn," Margaret said. "I'll watch the girls."

"No thanks. I can't ski."

"Of course you can, it's easy," she insisted, refusing to take "no" for an answer.

I thought for a moment. "I guess there is something I need to tell you. I'm two months pregnant. Since I've had two miscarriages, I try to be careful during the first few months. I didn't want to mention it because we haven't told the children yet. We think it's best to wait awhile."

"Oh, I'm sorry," she said. "I envy you. Our three boys are adopted. Teresa is our own. Unfortunately, I cannot have any more children," she said sadly. "I'll be very careful to keep your secret."

Teresa, hearing her name mentioned, suddenly realized she was hungry. "Children are like that," Margaret said. "Mention their name and they show up wanting something." She called out to the others, "Picnic time!" They came running, toweling themselves dry on the way. We sat around on blankets enjoying the feast and hearing of their feats on the water—and in the water.

"Does the boat skipper ever get to water ski?" I asked Tom.

"Actually, I do. Margaret is great at maneuvering the boat. She gives me a break now and then."

"After lunch," I volunteered, "I'll watch the girls while you take a spin."

"Righto," he said. "Then it will be time to trailer the boat and head home. We need to get the littlies into bed early. Tomorrow is Christmas."

Paddling with the girls in shallow water, I thought about the different ways Americans and Australians celebrate Christmas. In the States, we would be frantically rushing around shopping, wrapping and decorating. Here, Christmas was summer holiday time.

The next morning we all dressed in our best to attend church. Afterwards, the children rushed in to change clothes and headed for the pool. Tom fired up the barbecue, another new custom for us. Steak, chicken, shrimp, vegetables, chips and fruit provided a heavenly feast. Just when I thought I could eat no more, little Teresa leaned against my knee and looked up at me seriously. "We're going to have Christmas Pudding," she confided.

"Wonderful," I enthused. Not wanting to admit that I didn't know what Christmas Pudding was, I gathered up the empty plates and went into the kitchen to see Margaret. "Teresa told me about the Christmas Pudding. I've read about it in stories, but I've never seen one."

"It's a tradition," Margaret said. "I guess the best way to describe it would be a steamed fruit cake served warm with custard sauce. The kids love it as a special Christmas treat. I have it steaming now. It will be ready in about a half hour."

"Let me help you clean up the dinner dishes while we're waiting."

"Jolly good," she said. "After the pudding, there is one more place we want you to see. It will be good to have things cleared away before we leave."

The Christmas Pudding was a great hit with both families. "Mom, I'm glad we came to Australia," Skippy said, licking his spoon.

While everyone was finishing up, I changed sauce-covered Pam and Jackie into clean clothes. Thankfully, they had eaten the pudding with their bathing suits on.

"Can Teresa ride with us this time?" Tia asked. With a little shuffling, we arranged for Tom to take the boys while the girls and Margaret rode with us.

"We're going to Eungella Rain Forest National Park," Margaret explained as we chugged up a steep twisting road. "It's so much cooler in the mountains on a day as hot as this." As we climbed higher, we passed lush jungle growth dotted with the brilliant-colored tropical flowers. Finally, we reached the park. The children tumbled out to explore. We wandered along behind them, listening to their comments. Most of them were preceded by "golly," "gee" or "wow" with American accents, and "beaut," "blooming" or "jolly good" with Australian accents.

"Mom, look at those beautiful orchids," Mickey pointed up to purple orchids growing along a high limb.

"Mom! Dad! Look at those birds up there. They're parrots!" Tia shouted, gazing up at the treetops.

"Come on! Come on!" Skippy was signaling with his hand. "There are platypuses here swimming in a pool." We all rushed over to see these rare, found-only-in-Australia creatures. They had webbed feet and broad, flat tails.

"They use their tales to scoop up worms, shellfish and other prey from the bottom of streams," Margaret explained. "They're the only mammals that reproduce by laying eggs."

"That's not all," Tom said as we watched them glide through the water. "The male isn't as harmless as he looks. On each hind leg, he has a hollow claw. The claws are connected to poison glands. He uses them to scratch and kill his enemies."

Our absorption with the platypuses was interrupted by a wail from Jackie. Mickey had been carrying her around to show her the wonders of the park. He strode down the path with her, frustration written all over his face. "What's the matter?" I asked, as he held her out to me.

"He won't let me have the teddy bear!" she cried.

"It's not a teddy bear," Mickey fumed. "It's a koala bear way up in a gum tree. She wanted me to climb up and get it for her."

"Oh! Okay. It's all right, Mickey," I calmed him. Holding Jackie against my shoulder, I patted her back until she quieted down. Then I explained. "That koala belongs here. It lives in the tree with it's mother. You wouldn't want us to take it away from it's mother, would you?"

"No," she sniffled, laying her head on my shoulder, eyes ready to close.

Margaret looked at her watch, "No wonder she's acting like a tired two-year-old. It's way past nap time and almost dinner time. Tom, I hate to leave this place, but I think we should start back."

"I guess we'd better," Bill said. "There's is still packing to do if we're going to get an early start tomorrow."

Chapter Nineteen

A Corner of the Bay

BACK HOME FROM OUR WONDERFUL vacation, we concentrated on getting the children ready for school. Heeding Tom's advice, we enrolled Rusty in Marist Brothers boarding school on the west side of Brisbane. Tia, wearing sturdy black shoes and necktie, went to school with her other brothers, a transition that was very hard to cope with. Our little girl was away all day, and our oldest, away for the whole year.

Hoping to fill the void, Bill suggested a day's outing at the bay islands. "That sounds good," I agreed. "It's just too quiet around here. Pam and Jackie are lost without their big sister."

Hearing her name, Pam climbed up on my lap, "Are we going on a boat?" she asked, wide-eyed. I nodded. "And Jackie too?" I nodded. After a quick hug, she ran off to tell her sister the good news.

The following week, we stood on the Redland Bay jetty waiting for the morning ferry to Russell Island. I held Jackie's hand to keep her from getting too close to the edge of the jetty. She was as bold as Pam was shy.

The water, smooth as glass, rippled gently as the ferry discharged its cargo of spirited high-school students. Both boys and girls were dressed in uniforms, wearing hats, neckties and the same sturdy black shoes. They were carrying what looked like overnight suitcases. Laughing and joking, they headed for a bus that would take them to a high school eight miles away.

"Why are they carrying suitcases?" I asked Bill as he scooped up the girls and tucked one under each arm.

"Those are 'ports,'" he explained, stepping onto the deck of the ferry. "They hold all their school supplies and often weigh as much as twenty pounds."

I paused at the top of the ramp to look back. "Wow, that's a day's work before they even get to school."

The ferry skipper, Jack Noyes, smiled as he reached out to help me onto the boat. "Some of those kids walk more than a mile to the jetty every school day. Keeps them strong and healthy," he grinned.

The ferry was being loaded with bread, meat and supplies for the islands. When it was finally ready to sail, Bill led us through the cabin to a little deck in the back. We settled on a bench to enjoy the view. Watching the water ripple against the boat, I sighed. "It's so beautiful and calm." I turned to Bill, "How long will it take to get to the islands?"

"As the crow flies, it's a three-mile trip that takes about an hour," Bill answered. "That includes the stops it makes at different islands." He pointed ahead to floating yellow buoys. "Those buoys mark the channel because it zig zags around shallow mud banks. They call this area 'the W's.' The skipper told me it's tricky to get through the W's without running aground on a mud bank."

"Is it dangerous?" I asked, hoping I wouldn't have to swim back.

"No!" he laughed. "Mr. Noyes has made this trip so many times, he could probably do it in his sleep."

Twenty minutes later, as we rounded a bend in the channel, we saw Karagara Island, the first stop. The people at the jetty were waiting for the biggest event of the day—the latest news with their meat, bread and mail. Jackie, sure that we were getting off, tried to wiggle out of my arms. "Not yet," I told her. "Just wave at the people." While business was being taken care of, she entertained everyone with waves and dimpled smiles.

After the morning's news was discussed with the skipper, he turned the boat towards Macleay Island just across the channel. "Long ago, there used to be a lot of industry on these islands," my "information-expert" let me know. "Salt works, sugar cane, and pineapple factories to name a few."

When we pulled in at the jetty, it was Pam who told Jackie, "Not yet."

"Just one more island before we get to Russell," Bill explained to her. "The next one is Lamb Island. There used to be an oyster company there," he said as he quickly grabbed Jackie who insisted on trying to climb over the rail.

"No, no, this isn't Russell Island," he told her as she continued to squirm. When she settled down, he turned to me with more information. "Russell has eight miles of hard-packed dirt roads, and over thirty farms." He finished his report just as the boat pulled in to the dock.

"You've done your homework well. I'm impressed," I said, gathering up our things.

With a pleasant "G'day" from the skipper, we left the ferry and walked along the jetty. We helped the children down the steps and climbed a steep, red-dirt hill to the main road. A little further on, we reached the country store. A group of islanders were relaxing in the shade of the porch. They waved a greeting. Clinging to me with one hand for security, Pam shyly waved back. "They're waiting for their bread and mail," she announced, looking up at me. She had learned that on her fist trip to the island.

"Let's stop to say hello," Bill said, putting Jackie down to stretch her legs. The shopkeeper, Chris Wilson, recognized Bill and came out to greet us.

"I brought my wife over to have a look," Bill said, introducing us.

"You couldn't find a better place to live," Mr. Wilson said. Nodding toward one of the farmers sitting on the bench and using the more formal address (as Australians do), he asked, "Isn't that right, Mr. Edwards?"

"Fair dinkum," Mr. Edwards nodded his head. "I came up from Sydney. I couldn't stand the noise of motorbikes roaring past at all hours. I had to get away from the racket."

Mrs. Edwards, a motherly, white-haired lady, agreed. "I never want to leave. I love it here. Our daughter, Sheryl, who's nine, goes to the school over there," she pointed across the street.

Looking at the school, I noticed a big corrugated-tin storage tank like we had under our house. "Why do they have a water tank there?"

"That's the school's water supply. It catches rain water from the roof," Mrs. Edwards explained. I didn't want to ask, but I wondered why they didn't have proper plumbing.

Saying goodbye, we walked past farm houses made in the typical Australian style. Some were on stilts with wide verandas, corrugated tin roofs and water tanks. Everyone we met had a friendly wave and a pleasant, "G'day, mate!" the Australian greeting for, "Hi, friend."

Scooping up Jackie who was lagging behind, Bill went on with his facts. "There are no doctors living on the island. In an emergency, a launch is called to rush the patient over to the mainland. Someone on the island phones ahead to have an ambulance waiting. The ambulance speeds them to a hospital in Brisbane. They don't pay any taxes and are under no local authority. Besides, it's warmer in the winter and cooler in the summer than the mainland. What do you think about that?"

"Very interesting," I said, puffing a little as we trudged along.

By day's end, we realized that the biggest commodity of the island was peace and contentment. We thought of the roar of traffic as it passed our house in Clayfield. Could this be what we were looking for? Was this Bill's life-long dream of an island paradise?

In the following months we returned to the islands for family outings. We looked at farms that were for sale and became acquainted with some of the people. We read books on buying a farm. We dutifully tramped up and down fields, inspecting properties on Macleay and Russell.

"This farm has four acres of bananas," we were told by one agent.

"That's nice," I said politely. I had no idea how big an acre was or how bananas were raised. At each property, the "in's" and "out's" of its irrigation system were explained. But goodness, it had been raining ever since we arrived in Australia, so we wouldn't need to worry about that.

The number of water storage tanks and their condition was discussed. I wasn't a complete dunce about those since we had one under our house. I assumed the previous owner liked rain water for washing. Personally, I preferred city water, under pressure, straight from the tap. Occasionally, I get short circuits where my thinking is supposed to take place. Honestly, it never dawned on me that those tanks might hold the only the water available. I guess that's why they say, "Ignorance is bliss."

With each visit, we felt more at home. But there was still a lot to consider before we could make the final decision. Bill and I discussed the pro's and con's. One of the biggest factors was the new baby due in July. We were adding a special bonus baby to our half-dozen. I fussed about the prospect of moving. "I've been caring for an infant or expecting one every time we've relocated," I complained to Bill. "And, we've lived in twenty different places! From temporary housing, to base quarters, from station to station, state to state and country to country!"

"It has been difficult, hasn't it?" Bill sympathized with a hug. "Especially being alone in California when Mickey was born. You know, I would have come home from the Philippines if it had been possible."

"Thanks, Hon, I know you would have. I guess I'm just having pre-baby cravings. I've never made you go out at midnight for ice cream or pickles at 4:00 in the morning, but this time, I do want something. I want to have the baby here. We have room. We're close to the hospital, and we have electricity and running water."

Bill sat quietly with his arm around me. Finally, he spoke. "Is it the King's farm that's bothering you?"

I nodded. "It seems so rundown and needs so much repair."

"Then we won't buy that one," he assured me. "I wasn't too happy with it either. But there is another farm available. The last time we were over on the island, Mr. Noyes told me the Tower's place is for sale. It's on the main road up on the hill. He said it has the nicest house on the island. Would you mind taking a look?"

I sighed wearily. "I just remembered something. Our storage contract with the Navy runs out in another four months."

"That's right," he said. "In May, we have to notify them of our shipment address. The baby isn't due until July. If the shipment is sent here, it will be very difficult to move everything later."

The idea of unpacking and repacking cured my "wants." The only option was obvious. "Let's visit the Tower's place this weekend," I said.

When we got there, Mrs. Towers wasn't at home to show us around the house, but Mr. Towers filled the gap. He walked us through two large bedrooms, three small bedrooms, a dining room, living room, kitchen and bathroom (with sink and tub). "The WC is down there," he said, pointing to a little house in the backyard. He called our attention to the screened doors and windows. "A rare thing in Queensland," he said proudly.

Bill and I looked at each other holding a silent conference. We nodded simultaneously. The decision had been made. We agreed, with Mr. Towers, to swap our house in Clayfield, our van and 1,000 dollars for the farm. A handshake closed the deal. The children were thrilled. They dreamed of ponies and a place to roam. We arranged for our household shipment to be forwarded from the States, hoping it would arrive before the baby was born.

One misty morning in April, our furniture was packed onto the barge truck. It went ahead to meet us at the island. With mixed feelings, we closed our Clayfield house for the last time. "This is our last trip in our van," I said as we drove to Redland Bay. "I'm going to miss it."

"Who needs a van? We have a whole farm!" Mickey called from the back seat.

"Yeah!" everyone chorused. With great optimism, we boarded the ferry for Russell Island.

Chapter Twenty

Mr. and Mrs. Farmer

"Do you know what today is," I asked Bill when we finally settled down on the ferry.

"Sure, it's April 17, 1964. Oh, no!" He clapped his palm against his forehead. "I forgot! It's our 15th wedding anniversary!"

"Just think," I sighed, "most people would be planning to celebrate with a romantic candlelight dinner. Here we are, moving to Russell Island."

"Is that what's wrong?" he asked.

"We'll have a great celebration later. But I miss Rusty. He should be here. I can't help wondering if boarding school was the right thing."

"Well, it seems to be the Australian custom for eighth-graders. We do want him to get a good education, and we weren't sure how things would go on the island. At least he'll soon be with us for Easter vacation."

"I know, but it makes me sad that he's missing an important family event."

"There are drawbacks, aren't there?" Bill sighed. Then, looking for a bright note, he remarked, "at least the others are having fun, even if it is a little misty."

Mickey was leaning over the rail with a warning for Tia. "There are lots of fish down there," he intoned seriously, "and even huge turtles and sharks. So don't fall in."

She looked at him as if to say, "You're not fooling me."

Skippy was wondering out loud if he could swim faster than the boat. "I'd be there already," he boasted. Jackie and Pam, sensing that this trip to the islands was somehow different, were staying close to Mom and Dad.

"Do you know why the Towers are leaving?" I asked Bill.

"Mr. Towers told me once that he had retired to go to the island to farm with his son. But the son left for some reason. After his son left, he told me his wife wouldn't stay any longer. He said she threatened to leave—with or without him. His only choice was to give up rusticating and go back to the city. The truck that's bringing our things over on the barge will take their things back."

I looked out across the water. A refrain from "The Cremation of Sam McGee," one of my favorite poems, kept running through my head: "Why I left my home in the South to roam 'round the pole, God only knows…." We weren't wandering around the pole, but I understood the feeling.

Mickey cheered me up with some interesting information. "Did you know that Mr. Noyes leans back and steers the boat with his bare feet?"

Mr. and Mrs. Farmer

Bill laughed. "The only other time I've seen anyone do that was when I was here during the war. Things haven't changed, it seems."

"We're there!" Skippy called from the deck.

Mr. Towers met us at the jetty in an old, blue 1929 Willes pickup truck. We dubbed it "Rackety Boom" from one of the children's story books. Everyone piled aboard, and we chugged up the hill past the store to the farm. I have often noticed that there is a unique relationship between a piece of equipment and it's owner. Separating the two often means the equipment ceases to function, especially if it is as old as Rackety Boom. When Mr. Towers parked in the yard, Rackety Boom decided to retire. That was the last time it moved under it's own power.

Mrs. Towers, a motherly, gray-haired lady, greeted us from the top of the steps. "Please come in," she invited. "Let me get you a cup of tea while the men take care of the furniture." The tea had a cozy, calming effect after the misty trip on the ferry. When we finished our "cuppa" as she called it, she offered to show me the house. "Let's start with the kitchen," she said.

In the kitchen, a comforting warmth radiated from a large stove in a corner alcove. It was a type I had never seen before. She explained it was a slow-combustion stove. Lifting up the thick, insulated lids, she showed me the cooking surface and how to open the stove to add wood.

"As long as a fire is burning, there will be plenty of hot water in this tank," she said, pointing to one side of the stove. "You must leave the insulated covers down when you're not cooking. They keep the heat in and save wood. That's why the stove is called a slow-combustion stove."

She introduced me to the kerosene refrigerator. "It runs very well and has a little place at the top where you can freeze two ice cube trays." She bent down and pulled out a rack underneath that held the tank. "It has to be filled every few days," she explained. "The wick will need to be trimmed once in awhile."

Downstairs, she showed me the wringer-type washing machine and the "clothes dryer" as she called it. Actually, it was a clothes hoist out in the yard. Back upstairs, toddler Jackie climbed up on a chair to see the light switch. "No, no dear," cautioned Mrs. Towers. "When you switch that, the electric generator out in the shed goes on automatically."

I couldn't wait for them to leave. I wanted to experiment with all this strange equipment. Finally, our furniture was unloaded and theirs packed on the truck for the return trip. We waved goodbye and closed the door. We were at home—Mr. and Mrs. Farmer. "Well, what do you think?" Bill asked.

"I think it has great possibilities. At least we have cupboards in the kitchen and a large pantry. But I do see a great need for shelves and closets. Especially with our new baby arriving in three months."

Alas, there was no time to revel in our ownership. There were beds to be set up, children to bathe, dinner to prepare and two goats to be brought in from the fields for milking. It was getting dark. I turned on the light switch. Nothing happened. I tried another switch. Nothing. We didn't understand at the time, but rain water had leaked through a small hole in the shed roof and shorted out the electric system. Bill rummaged through the box of direction manuals on the pantry shelf. Carrying a crank handle and mumbling to himself, he disappeared into the generator shed to meet his first crisis.

Mine awaited in the kitchen. The fire had gone out. A prelude to countless nights of dinner congealing on a cold stove while tempers grew hot. The solution was simple. Remember to feed the fire. Digging back into my childhood memories, I recalled the basic idea of a wood stove: open the top and fill it with wood. How often to fill it, or the condition of the wood, had never been discussed. Green, dry, wet—did it really make a difference? After all, fires are pretty hot, aren't they? They'll burn anything, won't they? I had a lot to learn. I called Tia. "Would you please go ask Daddy if he knows how to build a fire in a stove?"